"MAY YOU DRINK FROM THE SAUCER"

"MAY YOU DRINK FROM THE SAUCER"

TIMELESS TRUTHS FOR AN EXTRAORDINARY LIFE

JAC ARBOUR

PROCEEDS
PRESS
2013

ProCeeds
Press

First Edition
"MAY YOU DRINK FROM THE SAUCER"
by Jac Arbour

© 2013 Jac M. Arbour, All Rights Reserved.
No part of the contents of this book
may be reproduced by any means without
the written permission of the publisher.

Published by ProCeeds Press, LLC
Hallowell, Maine 04347
www.jacarbour.com

Printed in the U.S.A.

ISBN: 978-0-9898927-0-4

Library of Congress Control Number: 2013915509

Edited by Dan Koon
Copy edited by Amy Chamberlain
Cover and book design by Carrie Cook

For more information,
including the philanthropic mission of ProCeeds Press,
please visit: www.jacarbour.com.

To my mother Patricia,

my father Michael,

and my sister Amy—

the first mentors I ever had

CONTENTS

FOREWORD

JAC ARBOUR'S INSIGHTS BELIE HIS years. His track record defies all normal expectations of someone his age. His book is a superb example of a self-help philosophy that will advance anyone's quest for higher achievement, so I am honored to write this foreword for it.

"May You Drink from the Saucer" will stretch your thinking about your own capabilities and provide inspiration for you to vigorously pursue the next level, regardless of your chosen endeavor. This work is a unique combination of lessons from self-help and historical greats and Jac's own philosophy of success, which started serving him well at a very early age. One of his best attributes in particular adds measurably to Jac's philosophy and, ultimately, his writing expertise: a hunger for knowledge accompanied by a voracious desire to learn how to do whatever he does *better.*

This book offers multiple principles backed up with tactical recommendations on how to use them for your best results. Whether it is about understanding success in more depth, setting goals and objectives, or communicating successfully with others, this book gives you results-oriented approaches that will make you think and act. The depth of this book is based on well-thought-out strategies for doing important things in an improved way.

Many years ago I learned that our success is based largely on the premise that it is not what we know but what we *do with* what we know that counts most. Great ideas are meaningless without proactivity. Vision without action is hallucination. I love to read a self-help book that offers sound ideas and recommendations for implementation, and this is such a book.

I would like to suggest that *"May You Drink from the Saucer"* is a book you will want to make notes in the margin of. Underline or highlight the things that resonate with you. I have many books that I have devoured and made a lot of notes in, and I will not loan these out or give them away. Each book simply becomes too valuable an asset for me to risk giving it up, as I refer back to each for continued input and inspiration. This might well be such a book for you.

My philosophy as a speaker and writer has always been to offer a combination of *thoughts that inspire* and *skills to succeed*. When I read a book that similarly impacts my thinking, I enthusiastically engage with it. This has been such a book for me, and it might be such a book for you. I hope it is, and that you grow significantly from your time with it.

Don Hutson, CPAE
CEO, U.S. Learning
New York Times #1 best-selling author
and Hall of Fame speaker

Before We Begin—
A Note from the Author

Each of our lives could be compared to a cup. Life, this cup, holds gifts and blessings, yet it also holds hardships and difficult experiences. All of these forever impress their marks on us. The elements that fill our cups shape who we are today and affect who we become tomorrow. Good or bad, each experience contributes to the wisdom we amass throughout our lifetimes, and it is this wisdom that leads us to prosperity.

When one says, "My cup runneth over," he or she is expressing a conviction that life has delivered prosperity of some kind. When the cup of your life is truly abundant with blessings and experiences, it overflows its edge and floods the saucer below. To drink from the saucer is to enjoy a superabundance of the good things in life—personal, emotional, professional, and spiritual. For me, this symbolizes the truest essence of a life well lived.

My hope for you is just this: *"May You Drink from the Saucer."*

PREFACE

ONSIDER FOR A MOMENT WHAT radio and television did for humankind in the twentieth century. The effects were transformational for our entire civilization. Think of the profound effect the Internet has had on our lives in recent years, even on those of us in the most remote places on Earth. A truly astonishing profusion of digital media allows us to ride a virtual tsunami of knowledge and viewpoints. One-third of the planet's seven billion people are connected to the Internet, a number that grew by more than 500 percent over the past decade.

Clearly, these advances in the exchange of ideas have allowed each of us near-instant access to a multitude of personal development and self-improvement books, videos, and other resources. Each of these carries the potential to shape our minds, influence our decisions, and affect our worldview's. Navigating the waves of inspirational perspectives while attempting to absorb and incorporate their wisdom, however, can seem daunting. A Web search of the words "self help," for example, returns more than one billion results, and "self improvement" over eighty million more.

"May You Drink from the Saucer" is a primer that distills the best of the broad array of self-help media. It shares lessons from historical and contemporary examples of success, and my own personal experiences with successful people and mentors in a concise read that provides you with clear, simple truths you can use. It is full of anecdotes and personal stories, both of mine and others, to give you real-life examples. As well, this book contains unique and practical techniques and exercises that enable you to evaluate yourself, identify your strengths, and develop the mind-set that will lead you to a life of *significance,* the exact definition of which will be up to you.

Certainly, this book contains principles that have been said before or written elsewhere. In fact, even two iconic books of the past century— Dale Carnegie's *How to Win Friends and Influence People* and Napoleon Hill's *Think and Grow Rich*—contain concepts of universal wisdom that were known thousands of years ago. This in no way lessens their value or diminishes the impact these books have had on the lives of millions of individuals throughout the world. Indeed, the positive influences of these books continue to this day. These men wrote for their times, but they built on wisdom that came down through the centuries. Confucius, Lao-Tzu, and others also wrote for their times and, no doubt, had their own antecedents and sources of inspiration.

The messages shared by many in the personal development field are so powerful that the sooner we can learn of them, the better. Our values, our perception of what is possible, and our foundational beliefs become hardwired at a young age. Wouldn't it be best if we were to make these time-honored principles for leading a life of significance part of this initial hardwiring, rather than having to rewire ourselves later on? The earlier in life we are exposed to the practical wisdom of how to attain meaning and value in our lives, and the sooner we are guided by it, the longer we will have to benefit from these principles and even build on them.

We have all heard someone lament, "I wish I'd known that when I was younger," recalling the growing pain associated with some learning experience. Whatever that person wishes he or she had known was probably carved into the pages of a dusty book. If only that book had been picked up, dusted off, and its lessons absorbed!

Reading is a surefire way to take life's learning curve and flatten it like a pancake: quality media can give us access to the knowledge and insights of people who have already "been there, done that." Opening yourself to the knowledge and experience of others through books, lectures, and videos enables you to stand on the shoulders, so to speak, of those who came before.

You will find a listing of invaluable self-development resources at the back of this book, including Carnegie's and Hill's. The wide array of resources in the listing is indicative of the universality of the principles you'll find in this primer, and I hope you will be inspired to look further into the works of these men and women. The messages they offer are timeless truths, and each has the ability to impact your life positively and powerfully as you strive for value and meaning.

Your chances for developing a life of value in any area—financial, emotional, recreational, or any other—are firmly anchored to *how you think*. How you think stems from what you believe. A daily habit of spending as little as fifteen minutes reading material that is positive and uplifting can produce noticeable changes over time—first in your outlook, then in your overall mind-set and belief system.

You will find quotations from renowned figures at the beginning of each chapter and sprinkled throughout. I strongly urge you to research the lives and works of these men and women. When a quotation resonates with you, make it a habit to research the person who said it; learn about him or her. Doing this will deliver you into entire realms of knowledge you didn't anticipate.

Dale Carnegie once remarked, "Don't you have more faith in ideas that you discover for yourself than in ideas that are handed to you on a silver platter?" This book has been designed with the hope of inspiring you to hunt for your own answers and think for yourself. It will give you places to begin and assist you in your search for practical, useful truths.

It is not the goal of this book to tell you what to do but rather to help you find your own answers—original to you, tailored to you, *by* you! This is why I refer to each chapter as a *consideration*; all I suggest is that you *consider* the information in each passage and then, ideally, apply the action steps to experience the benefits. If you find something helpful or insightful, use it and continue to use it. If after considering it fully you find that something does not resonate with you, then you can decide to discard it or set it aside to revisit later. Simply, this book has been written to inspire thought within you, to shift your perspective, and to prompt you to action. It was not written to give pat answers.

Your personal belief system should be one of your targets of study. Consider analyzing your beliefs and come to understand them intimately. Your mind-set is the unseen engine that propels most of your decisions and the lens through which you perceive your surroundings. Your mind-set affects how you view the world and what you think is possible. It also plays a major role in the development of your habits, which ultimately can either carry you toward your goals or trip you up every step of the way. Therefore, become curious about not only your own mind-set and habits but also those of the people you admire.

I have been fortunate throughout my life—in grade school, high school, and college and now in my profession as a financial planner—that I have met and received advice from intelligent, strategic thinkers, some of whom have attained remarkable levels of professional achievement and noteworthy accomplishments in their personal lives. You will be introduced to some of these people and share in their stories and wisdom in the pages that follow.

From these mentors I have learned that each of us, regardless of individual circumstance, is equipped with the ability to attain all our personal and professional goals, provided that we consistently apply our efforts to identifying and striving toward the objectives that are most central to us.

To my surprise, I have also learned that some people neglect sound advice and profound wisdom while knowing full well that taking it to heart and implementing it would forward their development. I ponder the reason for this conscious resistance to growth each time I witness it. Although the specific reasons are individual to each person, I have come to believe that, in all circumstances, it is crucial to consider how the *inner you* perceives opportunity and possibility, because this is actually where action (or inaction) begins.

What do I mean by the "inner you"? I have yet to meet someone who does not have an internal *something*—intuition, an inner voice, instinct, an internal compass, a gut feeling, a hunch, or something else—that tells him or her whether certain actions are leading closer to or farther away from his or her goals. Human beings have an inner voice, as I choose to call it, which gives us guidance. Some people do listen to this voice, many choose not to listen to it, and some may not know *how* to listen to it. It could be said that this latter group finds it challenging to separate their thoughts and emotions from their internal voice. This book will help you distinguish your inner voice and make a habit of listening to what it is telling you.

My sincere wish is that this book will combine with the other resources available to you and create a powerful matrix, a foundation and inspiration that guides you to become a better thinker and a stronger doer and one who taps their full potential. It should help you to zero in on your true self so you can use your inner voice as your compass. Your compass will not only show you the right direction, it will develop in you a strong ability to identify the pieces of life that possess true weight—that lead you toward *significance,* as opposed to simply success. Remember, one can amass a great deal of money and material wealth and yet remain unfulfilled; however, a life filled with meaning and value is always a success.

My personal fascination with human potential has inspired me to investigate various people who have "made it big" in the gift we call life. While doing so, I've been fortunate to learn what each did to position him- or herself for such meaningful opportunities. In fact, much in this book is predicated on answers I received from these people when I asked them, "Knowing what you know now, if you could go back in time, what would you do differently to pack more achievement into a shorter time frame?" Or when I asked, "What would you tell a twenty-year-old to help him- or herself reach where you are now, but in ten years less time?" Another question I always make a point of asking: "If there is one single thing you wish you had known or wish you had done more of earlier, what is it?"

Regardless of whether the person I spoke with was an accomplished politician or business executive, whether a professional athlete or musician, highly noted author and speaker, successful parent, or couple enjoying a seventy-five-year marriage—each provided me with invaluable advice, often relating the words of the others. You will see that their recipes for a life of significance revolve around an ability to continually dream big and an ability to continually take action. Each stressed the importance of being able to stay motivated, passionate, and courageous despite any and all negative circumstances that might arise. Their words of wisdom laid the foundation for this book.

It is likely you will think some of the principles in the book are common sense or just plain simple. For example, I have been told on numerous occasions that a primary distinction between those who "get it done" and those who "wish they had done it" is the distinction between *doers* and *talkers*. Individuals who experience success in any endeavor are those who take action, every single day, over and over, with persistence and allegiance. Think how often it is that we have not incorporated into our daily lives the simple, basic lessons we learned in our childhood years or, worse, have forgotten them. Therefore, some of these common sense principles bear repeating.

My efforts have been to collect and build on simple yet invaluable core ideals. To that end, I have compiled twelve "considerations," principles for you to explore and implement. To illustrate these principles, the chapters include information that relates to some of the greatest political, personal, and business achievements in American history. As you continue to grow and search for answers, you will learn of many more prominent individuals who incorporated the following considerations and timeless truths into their own daily lives. May you too take these as your inspiration.

Make a sincere effort to understand yourself for the person you are, spend some time considering who you want to become, and then allow the stories and information in this book (and the many others out there) to guide you.

Jac Arbour
Augusta, Maine
Summer 2013

Consideration #1:
Hunt for a Life of Significance

The clock is running. Make the most of today.
Time waits for no man. Yesterday is history. Tomorrow is a mystery.
Today is a gift. That's why it is called the present.

—Alice Morse Earle

Timeless Truth: There is no such thing as dreaming too big.

I WAS SITTING AT MY DINING room table. It was my twenty-first birthday, a significant date in anyone's life—at least in this country—marking as it does the entrance to adulthood. Instead of hoisting my first legal drink with friends in a jam-packed bar, I found myself at home thinking about how I had yet to meet anyone from my own small world who had dreams, passions, and visions for the future that were comparable to my own. I felt a sense of desperation to find someone I could relate to and, much more important, someone I could learn from. I had so many questions—if only I could find the right person to ask. An unrelenting internal pressure was building within me to identify what my next steps should be, and fast. I was eager to know the principles that would work for me in crafting a successful life for myself, and I felt equally sure that I was compelled to share these theories with others once I had learned them somehow.

As I sat there on my birthday, pondering my situation, a sudden flash of insight brought a notion that put me at ease. I realized that, if I want to attain my own definition of meaning in life, I would need to actively *hunt for it*. I was hungry for answers, and I would feed that hunger by taking action.

Lesson 1: Don't Wait for It—Hunt for It.

Hunting is a proactive sport. You track your game rather than waiting for it to come to you. It is the difference between watching TV and surfing the Internet. Television is a passive medium. You can recline on a couch or easy chair, and the information will come to you. All you need to do is be there to receive it.

Imagine searching for something on the Internet. You are sitting up—leaning forward, even. Your mind is engaged. You select where to go next. You are on the trail of whatever it is you are after. This is analogous to the mental shift that I experienced on my twenty-first birthday. I made the decision to look vigorously for the answers I needed. My decision to hunt led me toward some life-changing answers only three months later.

> I was in my junior year at Bowdoin College, and basketball season was in full swing. It was Christmas break, and our team was in the middle of an exhibition tour to the Bahamas. Around ten o'clock in the evening on December 31, after one of our games, I walked into the Isle of Capri Casino with a couple of my teammates. I felt remarkably alive. The rest of the team was already there. Some of the guys were trying their luck at the blackjack tables while others were crossing their fingers at the roulette wheel.
>
> All night, the casino continued to hum, especially around one person at a table about fifty feet away. A densely packed group was hovering around one roulette table. My teammate

16

and I casually walked over to take a look and find out the reason for all the commotion. What could be so fascinating about a game of roulette?

As I approached the table, I could see that there was actually a velvet rope separating the swarming crowd from the player—yes, only one. I peered over the others in front of me to see the action. There sat a middle-aged gentleman smoking a cigar, toying with a mountain of black chips, and occasionally sipping from a glass of champagne. I was intrigued by the velvet barrier that kept anyone from drawing closer than ten feet. *Why the rope?* I asked myself. My interest became officially piqued after only a minute of watching him. Who was this man, and what made him important enough to deserve his own roulette table?

Now really determined to investigate, I edged my way as close as I could and nonchalantly chimed out, "Having any luck tonight?"

Still focused on the spinning wheel, the man smiled and replied, "Every now and then."

Wanting to engage in conversation with him, I continued to make small talk with the man behind the velvet rope. I felt I could tell, after only a minute of watching the way he carried himself, that he had not only wealth but also answers to the questions I had been carrying. The hunt was on.

Eventually, the man behind the rope hit on number 23, which paid off at 17 to 1. He had won more than ten thousand dollars on a single spin of the wheel.

"Not bad for thirty seconds' worth of work," I chirped over the rope.

My comment drew a chuckle, and after a few more minutes of my corny banter, the most transformative period of my life began. The man invited me to step behind the rope and try my luck. Little did I know I had hit the jackpot before I even took my seat. One minute I had been cordoned off from the action, just another face in the crowd; the next, I had talked my way behind the rope. Better yet, I had been invited.

Thus began the warm-up to one of the most influential conversations of my life. I have no doubt whatsoever that this opportunity was a direct result of the conscious decision I had made months earlier on my birthday, when I decided to follow my hunger and to hunt for answers. That is exactly what I had been doing since then, and now it was about to pay off under circumstances I never could have envisioned.

It was obvious from the bottles of fine champagne and his sizable wagers that this man had great monetary wealth. But his trappings of prosperity were not the only things that distinguished him. What set him apart—aside from the velvet rope—was both how he carried himself, which was different from anyone I had ever seen, and how he expressed an unquestionable sincerity when he spoke. As I said, I knew right away that I needed to become more acquainted with his way of thinking.

I have always subscribed to the belief that it is an individual's mind-set—a person's specific attitude and mental orientation toward life—that sets him or her apart. I also believe that a positive mind-set is what can unlock a person's inherent potential. I didn't care what the man from behind the rope did for work or how much money he made; I simply wanted to understand his mind-set.

I pulled $100 from my wallet and bought four $25 chips. Over the next four hours, as 2005 became 2006, the man and I played roulette. Much more memorable than the game was our wide-ranging conversation about life, education, school, success, dreams, family, you-name-it.

18

As we shared our stories, I became aware that the man showed a complete lack of self-importance and a calm humility. Utterly polite and soft-spoken, every request to the dealer was accompanied by "Please" and "Thank you." The focus was never on himself but on those around him: the dealer, casino staff, the crowd, and me. I thought to myself, *This guy is so successful because of what he is doing right now.* My opinion then, as it is now, is that he is a master student of Dale Carnegie's techniques and lessons about how to treat other people.

Hours passed, and it was early morning when the man, whose name was Philip, suddenly asked if I wanted to see an "achievement" of his. "An achievement? Sure," I said, and he told me I could invite a couple of my teammates who had been watching to join us. He explained that he wanted to take a walk down to the marina and show us his boat.

My teammates Tim and Antwan and I left the casino with the man from behind the rope, and the four of us began our short stroll to the marina. I wondered why he referred to his boat as an *achievement.* I had been on plenty of boats in my life. *Boats are toys for grownups, behind which you go tubing, wakeboarding, and waterskiing,* I was thinking. *They aren't achievements.*

We quickly arrived at the marina, and as we continued down the dock, I soon noticed that, the farther we walked, the larger the boats became. Eventually there were no more "boats"; all I could see were yachts—mega-yachts, to be exact. I looked around, becoming more and more interested by the second, to see which one was Philip's. Although all the vessels were impressive, in the last berth of the marina sat 127 feet of floating *palace*—the "achievement."

As we boarded, I almost had trouble comprehending what I was seeing. Philip gave us a complete tour of the gigantic yacht. It had several decks, an interior that was beyond luxurious, amenities that couldn't possibly be counted, a crew of eight, and private security personnel. The main deck had a breakfast bar finished in Italian marble, a living room with a complete entertainment center and a baby grand piano, a dining salon, and a full bar of exquisitely crafted mahogany. The furnishings looked straight out of a penthouse on Manhattan's Upper East Side. The deck below had four staterooms, each with its own bathroom of shiny marble and gleaming fixtures. Towels and toothbrushes had the yacht's name emblazoned on them. The sundeck featured a Jacuzzi and plasma TV. In other words, it had everything, and the attention to detail was complete. It was a home away from home, literally, but one fit for a king.

Before our tour ended, our impressive host sat the three of us down on the back deck and engaged us in another of the most empowering and transformative conversations of my life. One by one, he looked each of us in the eyes, then said, "Gentlemen, I have shown you my boat, and that I have experienced great success. However, I haven't told you how my life arrived here; I haven't told you how I did it."

Philip then laid out what I have come to regard as the foundation of exceptional behaviors and the directions for achieving extraordinary results. In fact, his words have become my solid beliefs.

"Anything in life is possible," he began, and then went on to describe his life's journey, including the obstacles he had encountered and how he developed the cornerstones of his unique mind-set. He ended with the following advice: If you want to achieve your wildest dreams, (1) you must firmly believe in yourselves, your abilities, and your goals, (2) you must discover your inherent passions and act on behalf of your purpose, and (3) you must dedicate yourselves to mastering the skills necessary to accomplish it all. He made it sound so simple, so black-and-white.

As our host spoke, I could feel the desire to live up to my potential becoming refueled and ignited. He discussed the importance of never allowing your own or someone else's doubts to defeat you, the importance of never losing sight of who you truly are, and the value of staying true to those who have helped you reach higher levels.

The most amazing part of our encounter may not have been Philip's yacht or obvious wealth but the fact that such a man took the time to explain to three total strangers— three young college basketball players from Maine, no less—the source of his success, his way of thinking. To me, the most intriguing part at the time was that I felt I was actually identifying with the mind-set of this man whose unbelievable success I had witnessed firsthand. Here was the first person I had met who demonstrated an ability to see his vision through to fruition, and I felt he possessed definitions of success and a level of motivation that mirrored my own.

When our big conversation ended, we stepped off the yacht into the early morning hours of New Year's Day. As I stepped off the boat, I was certain that I was on the path to all my hopes and dreams.

The short amount of time I spent with this man changed my life. His words and example sharpened my intent, strengthened my resolve, and validated my drive. Up to that point in my life, I don't recall ever having felt so motivated, so inspired, or so hungry for achievement. It's worth repeating that my life-changing experience that night occurred because of one thing: a decision to engage. I could have walked past this man's table. I could have disregarded the internal voice that pushed me to approach him. I could have been complacent and waited for opportunity to approach *me*.

You must consider trusting your inner self and actively hunting for your success. If you want to get behind the rope and inside the mind-set, you must be willing to hunt for the destiny that awaits you. What should be clear from this episode is that anything can happen, including things so positive you may be unable to imagine them.

So do it! Maybe there is someone in your life you want to talk to, a mentor you sense could help you. Ask him. Write to her. Do it. You will find that many people are only too glad to mentor someone with a sincere desire to learn. You want to learn from truly successful people, and the measure of a *truly* successful person is beyond what he or she has accomplished or built: it is how many other people he or she has helped to reach *their* goals. So if you get rebuffed, at least you have learned who would not be a good mentor. Move on. Be on the hunt for answers, and never hesitate to ask!

Lesson 2: Trust Your Inner Voice and Be Proactive.

When I returned home to Maine after meeting Philip and touring both his boat and his mind-set, I immediately searched the Web for his name. I was blown away by what I discovered: article after article describing how he is involved in philanthropy on a world-class level. I read story after story about how this man has changed the lives of complete strangers.

One compelling story explained how he led an international effort to help a family dispossessed in their country's civil war. As a result of the efforts of Philip's team, the family was able to relocate to the United States and granted the opportunity to create a new and rewarding life. The mother is now the manager of a condominium complex, and her two sons both attended college and earned their degrees. This family was given a new start because one man had the desire to take action and create change. He trusted his inner voice and allowed it to guide him.

After a few hours of online searching, I concluded that this man is definitely a doer, the "get-it-done" type. Apparently, his consistent willingness to trust his own instincts and his ability to act accordingly led him to remarkable levels of success in various arenas. I knew I needed to speak with him again. I was aching to learn more from this person.

Seventeen days after I had left the Bahamas and returned to Bowdoin College, finally a web search on Philip turned up a phone number. I immediately phoned his office in Florida. I asked his assistant to give him a specific message: "Please tell Philip that he changed my life and that I want to continue to learn from him."

She paused and replied, "OK, is there any name to go with that?"

"Jac from Maine," I said.

A couple of hours passed, and the telephone rang. It was Philip. I couldn't believe it. Once again, and so soon, I had the opportunity to speak with this brilliant man. He expressed a little surprise that I had contacted him, particularly that I followed up so quickly. I immediately explained the reason for my call, sharing with him that on arriving home a couple weeks earlier I had thoroughly researched his work. I excitedly mentioned that I was beyond impressed with his business acumen, but even more so with the philanthropic and charitable work to which he has dedicated his life.

I felt that this man was doing what I wanted to do and had reached a level of achievement that I wanted to attain. Something deep inside compelled me to meet with him again, face-to-face. It was obvious to me that Philip had answers to the questions lingering within me. It was evident in everything he said to me the night I met him in the Bahamas. I needed to witness his mannerisms, his sincerity, and his genuine character at least one more time. I decided to cut right to the chase.

I asked, "What will it take to have one hour of your time, face-to-face?" I was asking for the world, knowing Philip had no time left in his schedule at the end of the day to shoot the breeze with me, a passerby. But what was the worst that could happen? He could say no, that's all. However, instead he said he'd think it over and get back to me.

A couple of hours later, my phone rang again. It was Philip. Within seconds, he asked, "Jac, what are you doing this Thursday?"

Philip explained he would be returning to the Bahamas that coming weekend. He had an obligation to fulfill for a group of musicians in Freeport and would be spending the weekend there on his boat. He invited me on the trip.

On my end, all I had to do to clear the way was to quickly convince my parents of the importance of the trip, persuade my coach to let me miss a couple of practices and the weekend's games, and be back in time for classes on Monday. Everyone resisted: my worried mother, my puzzled coach, and the dean, who insisted I not miss a single class.

It was like trying to clear customs without an identity, but I got the thumbs-up all around. It was a lot to work out in one day, but I knew I could not miss this opportunity for the world.

Desire and perseverance are responsible for many great outcomes. We must, like Philip, be a doer to get things accomplished. I made some calculated sacrifices that no one else could understand because I understood this was a trip I had to take, a trip that would have a lasting impact on my path in life. So I listened to myself, trusted my inner voice, then I did what needed to be done to make it happen. Doing so made possible an experience that would further empower me and fuel my hunt for significance. Taking the trip turned out to be one of the best decisions I ever made.

If something resonates with you, if it *makes sense* somehow, embrace that feeling, nurture it, and then relentlessly pursue that thing. Instincts, gut feelings, your intuition—whatever you want to call it, it is a powerful resource. Nonetheless, each of us is capable of overriding these crucial guiding messages with our logical, intellectual, and habitual ways of dealing with life. A newborn baby instinctively cries to get food, sea turtles instinctively move toward the ocean after hatching, and *our* instincts tell *us* what to do, too.

One could describe a gut feeling as an insight that bypasses our reasoning capabilities and comes to us directly through awareness. Because modern life demands so much logical thinking and rational, carefully considered behavior, we may lose touch with the more intuitive aspects of our being and even shut them out. It is possible that doing so keeps us from becoming the people we want to be. It only makes sense, then, to give full consideration to the feelings and urges that resonate deep within you. Your inner voice is speaking. Consider listening to it.

Lesson 3: Learn to Fish

My journey started with a quiet, early-morning flight from Portland, Maine, to Fort Lauderdale. My plane touched down into a warm, Florida-style January day. As I descended the escalator in the terminal, I noticed a man near the bottom holding a sign reading "Arbour." I was then transported by limousine to the modern, glass-faced building that houses Philip's office. Philip came out to greet me, then walked me back inside so he could wrap up some last-minute items. While I waited, I was honored to speak with the president and other officers of the company.

We left the office and took a private elevator down to the back parking lot, where there was an empty canopy under which Philip's car was usually parked. The canopy made me wonder what kind of car he had, and I waited eagerly until I saw the large front end of a sedan appear from behind a row of hedges. However, the giant hood medallion with interlocking Ms left me clueless. Although it was of a make I had never seen before, I could tell that, like everything else Philip owns, it was nice—super-nice. I later learned it was a Maybach, the highest-end vehicle made by Mercedes-Benz; all I knew was that it was luxurious beyond any vehicle I had ever seen, let alone rode in.

The Maybach stopped right on the tarmac at the jetport, the doors swung open, and ten feet away was a private jet. I stepped out and reached into the trunk for my bag. "I'll get that," the driver said, and put his hand on the bag to prevent me from picking it up. *I could get used to this,* I thought.

As I climbed into the plane, I was warmly greeted by two attendants, an immaculate interior with plush leather seating, and a wide array of snacks and beverages. Again, this was luxury I had never experienced, and, my mind flush with possibilities, I was tasting my dreams. Before I knew it, we were landing at Freeport Grand Bahama International; we had been in the air less than thirty-five minutes. Soon, I was again aboard Philip's palace away from home.

For the entire weekend, I was privileged to experience this different world, the fruits of Philip's quest for significance. Everything was done for me: my bed was made, my towels were washed and hung, scrumptious meals were prepared for me, and I had entertainment at my fingertips. Although I enjoyed it all, I had something in mind more important than being entertained. I wanted to discuss life, values, dreams, and goals with Philip. That was the reason for my journey, and over the course of the weekend I had this opportunity again.

Philip gave me the priceless gift of explaining his detailed mind-set with simplicity and great clarity. Over the course of a dozen hours that weekend, he gave me the details of what it took for him to achieve such macro-level success in business, finance, and his personal and spiritual lives. At one point he looked me in the eye and said, "Jac, I want to share with you exactly what it took for me to arrive where I am today..." and then continued with his fascinating life story.

I did not realize it at the time, but near the beginning of our first conversation Philip had asked me some especially direct questions that were central to my subsequent time with him and to the advice he gave.

"What are the three things of which you are most proud?"
"Who are the three most influential people in your life?"
"What are the three most memorable events of your life?"
"What are the three saddest moments of your life?"
"What are the three happiest memories you have?"

In the days and weeks after the trip, I began to understand that he was discovering for himself what made me tick and what kind of person

I was. Was I mentally strong or mentally weak? How did I measure success? Was I someone who understood the gifts that life has to offer? Did I understand the gifts of life that hold true weight?

Later, I also realized that Philip had gathered this information about me before he dispensed his first bit of advice. This entire set of questions and answers took only ten minutes, but it enabled him to gear his advice toward the type of person I was at the time and the goals that were most central to me. If, even from all of his experience, Philip had declared, "You need to do A, B, and C to reach your desired destination," his advice may not have been applicable to me at all. So, my interest in philanthropy became clear to him. He understood that I had an inherent passion for business and a sense for numbers, and that I had a passion for personal development and self-improvement. Based on his findings, he gave me advice that pertained precisely to me, my situation, and what I wanted to achieve in my life.

As I look back, Philip's approach also affirms an extremely valuable truth: that *anyone* can attain his or her dreams. In order to do so, you first must know who you are, what you believe in, what you want to achieve, and how you want to achieve it. Through his questions, Philip showed me how to discover these things about myself.

Everything Philip said was rooted in his own unique and specific way of thinking, and while I was gaining a grasp on his mind-set, I needed assurance that my own version of thinking big was also acceptable. He then shared with me one of his personal beliefs: anyone can overcome any obstacle, and as one does so, one's dream becomes his or her reality, no matter how grand the dream itself may be.

My weekend aboard Philip's yacht amplified my thought processes about human potential and empowered me in my future endeavors. There is the well-known Chinese proverb, "Give a man a fish and you feed him for a day; teach a man to fish and you feed him for a lifetime." That's exactly what Philip did for me.

I recommend you clarify your own mind-set and goals by considering Philip's powerful questions.

For You to Consider and Do

If you believe success is about finding the pieces of life that have true meaning and learning to fit them together, and that life is about growing and learning about yourself and the world around you, I urge you to consider and then answer the following questions.

1. What are the three things of which you are most proud?
2. Who are the three most influential people in your life?
3. What are the three most memorable events of your life?
4. What are the three saddest moments of your life?
5. What are the three happiest memories you have?

When you are satisfied with your answers to each question, ponder your answers. Try to objectively evaluate what these answers indicate about you as a person:

A. What are you passionate about?
B. What is most important to you?
C. Do your current efforts direct you toward your desired destination? If not, what do you need to change in order to experience the results you desire?

Lesson 4: Stay Positive and Keep at It

The thought processes that inspire one person to achieve great feats can lead another to believe he or she will never reach the end goal. One habit you may consider adopting is to ignore the negative energy, news, and opinions that surround you and focus on the positive in your life. The truth is, we are all products of our environment, and of where we invest our time and attention. In our super-connected, fast-paced world, there are endless opportunities to become distracted from our purpose and our goals, and what's more, some of these distractions have a decidedly negative influence.

A negative attitude can grow out of the seemingly endless bad news churned out in the media. Buying into the idea that the whole world is "just getting worse" is literally too easy. Recall for a moment the content of last night's local or national news. Look at the headlines of today's newspaper. When you are standing in the checkout line at the grocery store, read the headlines that plaster the covers of weekly tabloids. Truth be told, we are inundated with negativity. It is all around us, because doom and gloom sells. Money in the pockets of publishers and broadcasters can mean a less-than-optimistic worldview for you.

This is why we must proactively hunt for the truths that will improve our lives and leave us feeling more optimistic about what lies ahead. Prepare yourself, because here is the crazy part: the minute it takes to read an article about the most recent scandal in Hollywood is the exact same amount of time as the minute it takes to read an article about how to position yourself for more meaningful opportunities. It's worth asking yourself which article will leave you feeling more upbeat about the world in which you live.

Consider changing the channel tonight to something more positive, such as a nature show or a morally uplifting movie—I'm serious. Consider ignoring the news headlines on your browser window that blabber about the most recent divorce in Hollywood and the millions of dollars someone is getting because of it, and redirect your attention to a website that discusses a leisure activity you are passionate about. Maybe ignore the newsstand on the street corner and read an inspiring book instead. If you need suggestions for reading material, there is a list for you at the back of this book. Even ignore the TV news for a week or two. Try it; it is worth the effort to see your brighter outlook strengthening your resolve.

I encourage you to *keep hunting* for the answers you desire until you find them. Ignore the distractions and negativity around you, and know that the answers to your lingering questions *do* exist. Although your journey ahead may appear long and the road bumpy, never give up. Allow yourself the opportunity to find out what you need to know. If you believe you will find all the answers and hunt relentlessly for them, you will discover all you envisioned and more.

Finally, imagine for a moment the will and desire that exist in the heart of a wild and hungry animal. These attributes are the animal's best friends during its search for a fulfilling meal. Your own will and desires affect your hunt in a similar manner. As long as your hunger remains, the search presses on. Do what it takes to remain positive, no matter what, and always stay hungry. Create for yourself an impenetrable optimism, dream big, and take action. Keep at it; it will bring your dreams to fruition.

Lesson 5: There Are No Impossible Goals, and There's No Time but Now

Albert Einstein said, "Once we accept our limits, we go beyond them," and of course there are many individuals who have done this in spectacular ways. Take, for example, Bill Gates, Warren Buffett, and Oprah Winfrey. Bill Gates, along with others who launched the Information Age, instigated significant changes in the world on par with the impact made by Johannes Gutenberg when he invented the printing press in the 1400s. Warren Buffett has been one of the world's preeminent investors for decades, a man whose investment strategies have been the subject of dozens of books. Then there is Oprah, who rose from wretched poverty and abuse to popularize her own intimate, confessional style of talk show and is now rated in many polls as the most powerful woman in the world.

What are the characteristics shared by these three extremely successful individuals? One could answer that each is financially wealthy, each owns businesses, and each is an original thinker. All of which are correct. However, fundamentally, each is simply a human being—each must eat, sleep, put their pants on one leg at a time, and do many of the same things that the rest of us do. In most respects they are no different from any of us.

What sets our examples apart is that they understand there is no hidden secret to constructing and living a life of significance. There are millions of people who have become ultra-successful and who have done so in a variety of ways in all manner of arenas. The blueprints for financial, personal, professional, emotional, and spiritual achievement already exist. Stop and consider the fact that you are capable of similar achievements.

Mr. Gates, Mr. Buffett, and Ms. Winfrey share other characteristics as well. All are professionally engaged in their *personal* areas of interest. In other words, each does what he or she loves. In truth, the fabulous wealth of these individuals is actually a byproduct of their passionate pursuit of their own interests combined with a desire to bring change to the world.

It takes a special person and a unique way of thinking to reach lofty heights. It's true that between most individuals and people like these three giants stand personality traits such as unrivaled motivation, consistent allegiance to a goal, and an uncompromising effort to create an extraordinary legacy. However, realize that what underlies these character traits is a roaring fire that burns deep within them, and *it is this passion* that generates such unmatched motivation. It is a fire that each one of us can find, stoke, and feed, then use to propel our endeavors. As French military commander Ferdinand Foch once said, "The strongest force on earth is the human soul on fire." Consider finding the fire within you. Once you do, continue to build it and let it roar!

People living lives of significance have fed their passion in life and are letting that passion guide them to fulfill their purpose: they set their goals, however big, by the demands of that passion. As they relentlessly pursue those goals, though, they are exhibiting another shared mind-set: they can envision the future results of their efforts, even when at the moment there is nothing tangible in front of them to prove their progress. Their mind-set includes the gift of vision.

Conversely, other individuals become easily overwhelmed or disheartened when they begin to dissect the criteria for becoming what is, in their own mind, "successful." One of the top reasons a person begins to feel this way is that he or she is visualizing, all at once, everything that must be done. To many, that picture is daunting. A mentor once gave me this pertinent advice: "Keep your approach simple, and take one step at a time." For example, he told me, when creating a business plan, if you can't fit it on the back of a business card, it is too complicated. Don't allow yourself to be daunted by the work ahead; if you become overwhelmed, simplify, but don't lose track of your goal.

As you keep it simple, consider that the answers to some of your questions are already within you. When you need more answers, you will go hunting and search out everything you need to know. The answers are there: you will find them in the people you meet, in a good old book, in a video, or somewhere totally unexpected. Of course, there will be times when your own life experience will furnish the answers you need.

Some people become overwhelmed when they compare themselves to others around them. Why compare yourself to your neighbor, the smartest kid in your class, your boss, your spouse, or the best player on your team? This is something that many people do, but of course it is senseless; it serves only to weaken your frame of mind. You will never be anyone other than yourself—why would you want to be? You are *you!* And you are rare. *You* are that special person with a unique way of thinking who can reach those lofty heights.

Say it: *I am rare. I am unique.* And now, say it again...

The significance your life carries comes from within you. Comparing your weaknesses to the strengths of others will place you in mental quicksand. You only need to consider what achievements *you* desire and seek them out because they are important to *you* and because they define what a life of value means to you. Don't let comparing yourself to others douse your fire. Instead, let the unique desires and interests that fuel your passion also dictate your goals, and nothing will be out of the realm of possibility.

For You to Consider and Do

There is one standard against which you should consider measuring yourself. That standard is your own personal potential. It is a worthwhile challenge to identify the potential that lies within you and then strive to uncover what that particular potential is actually capable of.

Let's imagine for a moment a few of the goals you may have. Maybe you want the job of your dreams, or perhaps you want to climb a certain mountain, literal or metaphorical. Maybe you want to be accepted into graduate school. Maybe you want to sail the Caribbean. Consider this: apart from your own mind-set, what person or thing is standing in front of you, restraining you, and forbidding you from doing so?

Consider asking yourself, "Apart from any logistical issues

or external limitations I may currently perceive, what would my potential alone allow me to achieve?" Ask this, then ask what you can do about it. Actively search for the answer. You will be surprised by what you find.

Consider the idea that the only glass ceiling in the world is the one you create as a result of your way of thinking. Because this glass ceiling is in your mind, it follows that you can make the choice to abolish it. This is surely easier said than done, but because our mind is indeed our most powerful tool, we simply must learn to harness its power to our benefit. We must direct it away from limitation and toward opportunity.

Bill Gates, Warren Buffett, and Oprah Winfrey are all human. Just as Warren Buffett will put on his pants tomorrow, so will you. Just as Bill Gates will eat tomorrow, so will you. Just as Oprah will sleep tonight, so will you. We all will do these things, and the truth is, we all awaken each day with a certain amount of potential. What will distinguish us is what we decide to do next.

There is no such thing as dreaming too big, and the time is now. You can't live your life twice. That may sound ridiculously obvious, but think about it. The amount of sand in the hourglass of your life is finite, and when the last grain of sand sneaks through the neck, there will be no hand to magically invert the glass to grant you more time. This is it... this very moment. Your time is now.

A couple came to my office to determine whether they needed to make any changes to ensure their long-term financial security. The clients were a husband and wife in their early sixties. Let's call them John and Anne.

John worked his whole life in a naval shipyard building frigates while Anne stayed home and raised their children.

Although their love for each other was obvious, John and Anne quickly displayed diverging perspectives about what to do with their financial resources.

Life appeared to be a black-and-white proposition for John, and he impressed me as a "my way or the highway" type of person, conservative and set in his ways. We sat at a table in my office, papers spread out before us displaying various options. John firmly asserted his view: their funds were best left untouched in their simple savings account.

As our conversation progressed, it became clear to me that John was the one who made the financial decisions in the marriage, not atypical for the family breadwinner. His primary concern was risk avoidance, and his strategy was basically this: Keep the savings where there is virtually no risk, and don't spend a dime unless it is absolutely essential.

Anne was soft spoken and more laid-back. She confidently rebutted her husband's argument, illustrating the lack of growth they would realize if their hard-earned money were to lie dormant in the bank. She could see the value in investing as a hedge against a possible medical catastrophe in the future, citing the effect such an event would have on their life savings. Both John and Anne wanted the peace of mind that would come from a guarantee that they would be able to stay in their home even if one or both of them should need long-term care.

I sat on the sideline as the conversation volleyed back and forth. John stubbornly stuck to his belief that long-term financial planning carries an uncomfortable level of uncertainty. Anne remained firm in her words and tone while stating that something needed to be done, and that in her mind doing nothing was the same as planning on future hardship.

Finally, Anne turned to her husband, looked him straight in the eye, and said in a loving but firm tone, "Honey, life is not a test run." She went silent, maintaining eye contact with her husband of almost forty years. John sat back in his chair, and a stunned look of realization came over his face. Anne's point was clear. And John understood.

What Anne could not have realized was how deeply her words resonated within me, too, and they continue to guide me today. Her declaration, simple as it was, seemed to reach across the table, past her husband's ears, and douse me in a refreshing clarity. For me, at that moment, they were an epiphany.

As they say, you have never seen a hearse pulling a U-Haul trailer. Even in the game of Monopoly, after you amass great wealth and all the material trappings of success, everything goes back in the box. What Anne told her husband is a timeless truth: When it is our time to go, we are not taking anything with us. Further, we are not on earth to avoid taking chances or to wait and see what might happen. We are here to live! Our time is finite, and we are here to enjoy the fruits of our labor.

If you want a life of meaning for yourself, consider that you are the force to make things happen, and only you can chase your dreams. No one else is going to do it for you, no matter how long you may wait. If your ship does not come into the harbor, then you absolutely must swim out, climb aboard, and get it moving.

In many respects, we live in a world where the most harmful limitations are the mental ones we impose on ourselves. With the proper mind-set, there are no boundaries or limits when it comes to our lives and the relationships we can forge, to the value we can offer the world, to the love we can share, the truths we can spread, the glory we can uphold, the integrity we can express, or the good we can do.

My great friend and philanthropic mentor John C. Bridge once told me that life equips us with the ability to *do it all, have it all, and give it all.*

For decades, John was president of one of the leading construction companies in Maine. After selling the company, he devoted his time and fortune to philanthropy, and today he remains as busy working for charitable causes as he was in his days as company president. His wife, Charlene, says that he is busier now than ever.

John graciously met with me one day in the boardroom of the Kennebec Valley YMCA, where he and I volunteer. During our conversation, he informed me that the ability to completely live life originates from *within,* specifically from our ability to choose, our freedom of will. As a result of this freedom, he stressed, we must hold ourselves accountable and continually make the deliberate and free choice to act on behalf of our purpose, to make our goals and visions a priority, and to make this pursuit of our goals and visions simply a way of life.

John pointed out that people who achieve greatness in life—that is, a life of true meaning by their own definition—do so not by taking action for only short spans of time. Figures from the past who achieved true greatness, in whatever field, he said, were motivated by a deep, burning desire to create change or to do something important, and then *deliberately created their lifestyle* out of that desire. (Perhaps this reminds you of the three mega-successes we've been discussing.)

A life of significance requires long-term commitment and dedication, ultimately strengthening one's allegiance to a purpose. In a cycle of success, the fulfillment that comes from living a life of purpose generates additional self-confidence, and this too makes one's purpose itself more rewarding and one's efforts more fruitful.

So, do you choose to *do it all, have it all, and give it all?* Do you want to apply your efforts now toward remarkable accomplishments, or are you content with waiting for less? Either way, the person who will determine the outcome is the person staring back at you in the mirror. If you are intent on living a life of significance, consider the blunt advice of Pablo Picasso: "Only put off until tomorrow what you are willing to die having left undone." In truth, none of us knows for certain when the sands of time will run out.

The time to act on behalf of your goals is now. Specifically, it is time to identify what you want out of life and what will bring the greatest meaning to you. We all must learn to enjoy the journey and live in the present moment while maintaining our awareness of future goals. It will behoove you to gain the ability to eliminate any and all negative or self-defeating thoughts from your mind and place yourself quickly back on track when necessary. It is time to learn to reject negativity from others, in word or action, and remove it from your life. And finally, it is time to define what significance means to you, in your own terms, not someone else's.

The remaining chapters of this book will help you to incorporate these lessons and to make the most of your time. *This is it.* Life is not a test run. You are in the homestretch.

CONSIDERATION #2:
LEARN WHO YOU ARE AND WHAT YOU ARE MADE OF

Do you wish to be great? Then begin by being.
Do you desire to construct a vast and lofty fabric?
Think first about the foundations of humility. The higher
your structure is to be, the deeper must be its foundation.

—SAINT AUGUSTINE

EACH PERSON ON THIS PLANET has a purpose. Have you become well acquainted with a feeling that resonates deep within you? Is there something that you have forever felt passionate about? Take a moment to look inward and ask yourself if you have identified your own purpose. Do you have it clearly in focus? If so, say it out loud.

And now, write it down. The first goal of Consideration 2 is to help you to visualize your purpose and to see it with pristine clarity. The second goal is to promote your moving forward in life by taking actions on behalf of this purpose.

Did you know that the average number of years an employee stays at a job is four? Some researchers cite that a person will undergo seven career changes during his or her working life. It's hard to imagine how a person transitioning at this rate can possibly manage to build a knowledge base that allows him or her to master a particular set of skills. So why do people change careers so frequently?

Perhaps it is due to boredom, or maybe people are chronically dissatisfied with their financial compensation. Possibly it is because many jobs are simply not what the employee had envisioned. Consider that, at its root, this dissatisfaction may instead be due to the lack of passion most people feel for what they are spending their precious time doing. They may be doing work entirely divorced from their own sense of purpose, whether they know what their purpose is yet or not.

TIMELESS TRUTH: YOU CAN DISCOVER YOUR PURPOSE BY FOLLOWING YOUR HEART.

The high employee-turnover rate underscores the importance of identifying a career you are passionate about and work that allows you to feel fulfilled. I often share the story of how I discovered the career in financial planning that I enjoy so much and how I began my business at such a young age. In fact, it was a very simple route—not necessarily easy, but certainly simple. I believe my story illustrates that our hearts hold many answers, and they can truly be the maps that guide us to success. Consider that you have the ability to discover your purpose and turn it into your career path, just like millions of others have done.

> When I entered college, I had my sights set on a career in dentistry. The idea of becoming a dentist and having the independence of my own dental practice seemed like a good path to take at the time. By my junior year, however, I had begun to notice that I had no real passion for organic chemistry, physics, or any other course, in fact, required for such a career path.
>
> I remember a few of the conversations I had with my mother discussing my plans around that time. "Jac," she finally said during one of them, "are you sure you want to

go into dentistry? You're good with numbers, you're good in dealing with people. You've always liked dealing with money. You've always liked watching it grow. You're intrigued by entrepreneurialism and investments. Why don't you get into banking or financial planning?"

There I stood, so far along in my science curriculum that I was bound and determined to finish it (and I did), although I no longer found it enjoyable. My mother's words stopped me in my tracks. It dawned on me that I had been focusing my course of study on what I believed other people would approve of rather than on that for which I had a passion. Clearly, my own particular aptitudes, my talents and my skills, would be better suited for something outside of the medical field, but I wasn't making the connection that what I enjoyed was also that which I naturally did well.

My mother was not the only person who was asking me such questions and pointing to the (in retrospect, blindingly obvious) fact that I should be doing something different from studying to become a dentist. I was aware of it, too, but I didn't know that yet. My heart and my inner self urged me to make a change a million times if they did once. Like so many people, I was simply not listening to my inner voice at the time.

Going to a good college alongside the sons and daughters of the wealthy class, many of whom were tracked for careers in law or medicine, had made it easy for me to believe I should be preparing myself for a similar career. Lacking a strong interest in my own chosen subjects of study seemed wrong, though, and I finally realized it is far more important to be doing something I love than anything else, even something viewed as honorable by other people. In reality, I knew it wouldn't require being someone I wasn't to become successful by any definition.

I began to read more newspapers and magazines about finances, the stock market, investing, and the like. I began funneling more of these things I naturally loved into my career path. After college, I soon joined forces with my current business partner and began selling life insurance, annuities, and long-term-care insurance. I loved selling, and I was fortunate enough to taste success right away, qualifying for the Million Dollar Round Table in each of my first four years in the business. I attribute my business successes to a number of things, but at the top of the list, the most fundamental reason is that I decided to spend my time doing something for which I have an inherent passion.

Our primary challenge in uncovering our purpose may be to ignore what everyone around us tells us we should or could be and learn to trust ourselves. It's not easy, but it's simple. Listen to your own instincts, your own internal notions, and then act on what you learn from them. If it ever seems as though you are unable to identify the answers within you, have faith that your heart will guide you to what you need, and keep asking.

Consider tapping into the passion that lives deep within you. Nurture it, cultivate it, and allow it to blossom. It is its own reward, and ultimately, it will be the source of your satisfaction and your success.

For You to Consider and Do

Here is a mental training exercise that has facilitated my own internal growth. It can assist anyone in discovering his or her passions, and potentially, it will help you find your life's purpose.

This exercise is fairly straightforward: for the next two weeks, every morning when you wake up, even before you open your eyes, you will ask yourself the same simple question. Exploring this question can harness an indescribable amount of power for this reason: it is probing for inner truth. And the only person who can answer this question is you.

1. The first thing in the morning for the next two weeks, ask yourself: "If I could open my eyes right now, step out of bed, and do anything, go anywhere, or be anywhere in the world, what and/or where would it be?"

2. Allow your clear mind to roam at length. Leave your eyes closed and let your imagination take over. While doing this, remember the first Timeless Truth: *There is no such thing as dreaming too big.*

3. After you are done, open your eyes and write down all your thoughts, in their entirety and in detail.

Ask yourself the question and record your answers in a journal every morning for the next two weeks. Keep it in a private place if you like. At this point, the key is to keep recording your hopes and dreams. It is not necessary, and may not even be desirable, to share your answers with others. This exercise is about you—more precisely, the *inner* you.

4. At the end of the two weeks, take some time to sit down and review all your entries. After you do this review, you will need to make one last entry; this entry will serve as a summary of the past two weeks. Reflect on the things you have written and look for the commonalities among the entries recorded on different days. Write down the desires that overlap.

5. Once you have identified the overlap, you have taken the initial step toward identifying your inherent passions. Ponder the recurring themes and desires in the answers you recorded. The ideas you had on multiple days, the things that kept repeating themselves over and over, the places to which your mind brought you—these are the places and things that you need to consider how to make a part of your day-to-day reality.

I encourage you to repeat this exercise every three months or so. It will help you to stay honest with yourself and to better understand your interests and your wants and desires. When you truly know what it is you want to squeeze out of life, you can begin to see what you should do. Then you can start to implement plans of action, and results will follow. That is simply the nature of the game.

Consistently attempting to understand yourself and your direction in life is the key to staying on course. It is easy to wake up each morning, jump out of bed, and start and end your day without ever really stopping to think about the direction in which your actions are pointing you. Why? Because we are human and, therefore, creatures of habit.

We naturally find comfort in familiar actions and inevitably create comfort zones that are hard to escape because they become so firmly established. Frankly, it is just easier to amble through life practicing redundant actions and reliving familiar situations that, due to repetition, we are comfortable handling. We must not forget that, for most people, experiencing their own passions, desires, and dreams will lie just beyond the threshold of their comfort zone. Therefore, consider stepping outside your comfort zone, and into the place where your possibilities exist.

Our deepest roots are our purposes and passions. As with the roots of a tree, we cannot see them unless we unearth them, and that is the purpose behind the exercise above. But, while unearthing the roots of a tree will eventually harm it, exposing your roots to self-contemplation and reflection will nourish them instead.

Vince Lombardi, legendary football coach of the Green Bay Packers, once said, "Success demands singleness of purpose." If this is true, it is safe to say that we cannot fully realize our greatest ambitions without identifying our purpose. In addition, it would be accurate to characterize success as something that originates at our core, our roots. It is only when you are fully and continuously aware of your purpose that you will be able to consistently act on behalf of it.

Consider investing the time to unearth your roots and to examine your potential. I can unconditionally promise that, if you earnestly strive to understand yourself for who you are, to gain insight into who you want to become, and do so consistently and with vision, you will find fulfillment. It is one of the greatest blessings in life to have faced who you are and to have subsequently realized what makes you feel truly fulfilled. Once you know what you want, approach it enthusiastically, and never second-guess your ability to attain it in its most complete form.

In all, the important first step toward living a life of significance is to become well acquainted with the components of the *inner you*— who you are at your core, apart from what you do for a living or what you do on your weekends, what car you drive, what you have for a home or wear for clothes, or the status you hold in your community. The inner you is not your name, your hair color, your physical shape, or even your face. Some of us are aware of our inner selves and know how to follow our hearts. For others, the *inner self* is only a vague concept. However, there are key components with which we are all familiar that represent our inner selves.

And this brings us to the next Timeless Truth:

TIMELESS TRUTH: YOUR MORALS AND CHARACTER GIVE RISE TO THE REPUTATION YOU'RE BUILDING AND THE SUCCESS YOU WILL EXPERIENCE.

Morals are the roots of your character. Character is the root of your reputation. Reputation is the representation of who you are to the world around you. By exploring and understanding these three components, we can actually strengthen our connection with our inner self and increase our awareness of our true nature. I became most aware of these components through a special relative of mine, my great-uncle Babe.

His real name was Hector, but to me and the rest of the family he was Uncle Babe. He was my paternal grandfather's brother, and although I never knew my Grandfather Clement, Uncle Babe was a constant in my life for many years.

Uncle Babe lived across the country from us, in Kalispell, Montana, but when we were growing up he was a frequent spectator at many of my and my sister's games, as well as those of my cousins. He was a wonderful photographer and captured many memorable sports moments for all of us.

Rather than fly back and forth between Maine and Montana, Uncle Babe would often take the train so he could enjoy scenic America as it rolled past. He would stop in New York City first, to be treated for his non-Hodgkin's lymphoma, and would then continue on to Maine to visit the family. I always found it inspiring that my great-uncle took such an active interest in the lives of his grand-nieces and grand-nephews, particularly because he lived half a continent away; but that was just our Uncle Babe.

Uncle Babe battled non-Hodgkin's lymphoma for years. At one point it looked as though the cancer had gone into remission, and he was given a clean bill of health, but at his next appointment six months later, he learned that it had spread throughout his body and that nothing could be done. He lost more than fifty pounds, turned as yellow as a person could be (from jaundice), and had difficulty walking, yet he refused to miss out on a final family gathering so he could take pictures, eat Maine lobster, and be with the family he loved. Although Uncle Babe knew he was going to die, any fear he might have felt remained out of sight to all of us, and his uplifting, jovial personality and his sincere interest in what all of us had going on in our lives were all we saw. The best of Uncle Babe had not diminished one bit, even as his flesh and bones were wasting away.

Before his passing, I initiated a project to support the morale of my Uncle Babe and all the supporters around him. My endeavor soon became known as "The Bracelet Project." I had 500 rubber wristbands made: they were blue, to represent water, which is essential to life, and they had "All of us for Babe" inscribed on them. There was also a special inscription on each bracelet that told his family relationship to the wearer, such as "Dad" for his three children or "Uncle Babe" for his nieces and nephews. Within a month, there were hundreds of people across the country wearing these bracelets: family, friends, associates—this man touched many lives. We put together a PowerPoint presentation of photos of all the people wearing their bracelets and set it to music. Seeing just how many people were rooting for his recovery was a moving and remarkable experience.

My Uncle Babe's tangible dedication to his family and his far-reaching and uplifting influence inspired me to send him a personal message about a month before he passed: *"It does not matter if the fight is won or lost, but rather how the fight is fought, that determines a man's character, a man's honor...and you are a champion."*

Uncle Babe inspired me to investigate the specific elements of a personality and attitude that make such a person strong enough to withstand adversity, in this case the ravages of a terrible disease, and yet to remain whole and maintain an incredibly successful personal life. A person who cultivates such a personality, to my mind, can be assured of attaining much in life. Today, he still inspires me and influences my life, and I hope his story will do the same for you.

Morals: Drivers of Action

Morals and morality are fundamentally the distinction between good and bad, right and wrong. The words come from the Latin *mors/moris,* meaning "custom" or "proper behavior." A society discovers that certain behaviors among its members tend to influence the society positively, and others affect it negatively. Out of such observations and beliefs grows the moral code of a society. From an individual standpoint, morals can best be described as the collective intangibles residing in a person's subconscious that give rise to intentions, decisions, and actions.

Morals are the driving forces behind what choices we make and the reasons why we make them. Morals guide our thought processes and our actions, including how we treat others. And although our morals themselves may be intangible, they reveal themselves quite visibly in our character.

Character: The Moral Quality That Defines a Person

Our character is composed of the qualities that shape who we are and what we show to the world. Such virtues as courage, honesty, integrity, trustworthiness, and loyalty, or lack thereof, define the character of an individual. Cavett Robert, founder of the National Speakers Association, once defined character as, "The ability to carry out a worthwhile resolution long after the mood in which it was made has left you." That said, your character underscores how you approach life at all times, even in the heat of the moment or when behind closed doors. It is the invisible, yet somehow tangible, representation of yourself that is perceived by those who come into contact with you.

For You to Consider and Do

To explore your own character, take a few moments to consider the following:

- Are you untrustworthy, or are you a person of your word?
- Are you indifferent about the truth, or are you dedicated to it?
- Are your words and actions troublesome, or do you act with integrity?
- Are you a pessimist or an optimist?
- Do you tend to make people upset, or do you make people laugh and feel lighthearted?
- How often do you tell those you love, "I love you?"
- Do you take the things you have for granted, or do you count your blessings?
- Do you give for the satisfaction of giving, or are there strings attached to the good deeds you do?

Truthfully answer each of these questions, and write your responses in a journal. Then read over your answers. Each question has an answer that society would generally categorize as either negative or positive. But how does society correctly categorize these answers, and how do we know which answers are positive? Your morals—the driving forces behind the decisions you make and on which your actions are based—will give you a pretty good sense.

So where do your answers stand? Are they on the positive side of the list, or do your answers fall into the other category? With these questions in mind, remember that your character speaks louder than you will ever be able to with your voice.

Your character is seen by everyone. It is constantly on display, even when you don't think people are looking. As an example, visualize your best friend. He or she could be in the next room or on the other side of the globe, it doesn't matter. See this person in your mind. When you think of your best friend, what you see is his or her character. Everything that person has ever said to you, done to you, or done for you is an expression of this thing we call character.

Therefore, it is worthwhile to consider how your character is built. Ask yourself: "How do my friends and family view me when I am not around?" Ask yourself what morals define your character, and whether your character includes all that you want it to. Consider that people always see your character, which is why your character constructs your reputation.

Reputation: The Integrity of One's Character as Judged by Others

Character is like a tree and reputation like its shadow. The shadow is what we think of it; the tree is the real thing.

—ABRAHAM LINCOLN

Like the tree and its shadow, your reputation often precedes you. As unfair or unfortunate as it may sound, people who have never met you, who have never shaken your hand or looked you in the eye, will sometimes form their opinion of you based solely on your reputation. Reputations, positive or negative, are things that tend to stick with you. Therefore, consider this: Your reputation is like wet cement, but only for a time. You have the chance to form it into just about anything you want, but, as we all know, cement will eventually harden and take its permanent form.

One of the best ways to make a positive impression and forge a solidly favorable reputation is to remember that in any given interaction you are evaluated as being either a resource (helpful) or a burden (a hassle). Positive people are most often considered resources and tend to contribute a helpful spirit to any relationship.

None of us is in total control of our reputation, and whether we like it or not, our reputations are continually available for inspection. What we can do, however, is work diligently to manufacture a strong foundation so that our repute can withstand the pressures that will inevitably be placed on it. Consider building your reputation to withstand any storm. Build it carefully with bricks of genuine character cast from strong moral fiber. Build an impeccable foundation. If you do, your reputation will withstand any storm of fate—or ill will—that blows through.

TIMELESS TRUTH: ATTITUDE IS EVERYTHING.

Attitude: Your Mental Approach to the Game of Life

Nothing can stop the man with the right mental attitude from achieving his goal; nothing on earth can help the man with the wrong mental attitude.
—THOMAS JEFFERSON

If your morals, character, and reputation are the foundation as well as the form and style of your house, then your attitude is a light that shines from its windows. Is your attitude a positive light under which everything flourishes? Or is it sometimes the cold light of negativity under which dreams *shrivel away and die*? Luckily, we are each the master of our attitude. Because what happens to us in life generally has less of an impact on us than how we respond to it, a positive attitude can give us the gift of incredible resiliency. I once heard that attitudes are contagious; ask yourself if yours is worth catching.

A positive mental attitude inspires one to ask *how* something can be accomplished rather than say it can't be done. Consider being the person who inspires others to acknowledge their own strengths and talents. Be the person who shares with others the philosophy that anything is attainable, that there is no such thing as dreaming too big. As best-selling author Don Hutson often says, there is no such thing as unrealistic goals, only unrealistic time frames.

If a life of value and meaning is your goal, your attitude must be a positive one. The character evaluation in the previous section (For You to Consider and Do) will give you a sense of where you stand. If it left you on the negative side of the ledger, there are probably some things you need to work on. It is a fact: if you were honest with yourself when you answered those questions and considered those ideas, you have already begun your work. Acknowledging the areas that need improvement enables you to begin making the necessary changes. Remaining in a state of delusion or denial only prolongs the negativity.

So, what do you do to improve your attitude if it is not as positive as it could be? For starters, consider again that your foundation is your morals, and therefore they are the precedent for the decisions you make. The decisions you make affect your success. The more success you have, the easier it is to be pleased with the results entering your life. The more you receive of what you strive for, the easier it is to have a positive outlook on the future and the world around you. Therefore, it is easier to have a more desirable and upbeat attitude.

Luckily, your morals are not fixed in stone. You *can* decide to change them and actually do so if that's what you truly want. The choice to improve your morals opens the door to better decisions and a more virtuous life, a better, more genuine character, an improved reputation, and a more positive attitude—all necessary for the attainment of your goals.

For You to Consider and Do

1. Become more aware of your decision-making ability. Daily, you make dozens, maybe hundreds, of decisions: whom to hang out with, what to eat, which computer to buy, what to wear, what to watch on TV, and so on. These are all factors that impact the person you are continually becoming. These decisions have effects that follow. For example, the information you choose to expose yourself to (such as this book) affects what you think about and how you think about it. Therefore, ask yourself why you tend to make the choices you make and then assess the quality of your decisions accordingly.

2. Strive to become mindful of your decisions while making them. Every now and then you will be faced with situations that test your moral values. If you have made a habit of mindfulness in your everyday decision making, you will have much clearer views of situations when they come to "crunch time." You will therefore be more likely to make decisions that positively influence your long-term success.

3. "Play the movie to the end." This is something a good friend once told me. When you are faced with a dilemma, try to visualize what the sequence of events and the result would be depending on which choice you decide to go with.

For example, say you are faced with making an important decision. Ask yourself what all the potential outcomes are and what they would mean for you and for others involved, then ask yourself: *Is there more good than bad that can result because of one of these decisions?* If so, go with that one. Sometimes, even the best option is not extremely favorable. Be sure to explore all possibilities before making any final decisions. The key here is to assess based on the facts and on your applied moral code, not based on emotion or impulse, both of which can sometimes get the best of us.

Author Jim Newton, who wrote the book *Uncommon Friends,* reminds us that *what* is right is more important than *who* is right. If we keep this in mind, we will usually make higher quality decisions.

4. Build a T-chart. Do it on a piece of paper or in your head, whichever works best for you. On paper, one column should be titled "Pros" and the other "Cons," with a line down the middle of the page separating the two columns. T-charts worked for Benjamin Franklin hundreds of years ago, and I can assure you that this method still works to improve decision making.

5. The 24-Hour Rule. It is usually the best policy not to make knee-jerk decisions on important issues. Another good friend shared with me the value of not making any difficult decision without first sleeping on it: the 24-Hour Rule. Putting a decision to rest for a period of time allows for a calm, rational reflection and creates distance between an impulsive reaction and the final choice. This "incubation period" works.

6. Trust your intuition and game plan. Once you find an effective way to make solid decisions, stick with it. However, always acknowledge variability in the way a given decision might be best approached. Familiarize yourself with your

own attitude and ability to choose and with the tools that can help you. Learn what works for you now and what does not. While choosing, remember step 2: be aware of your decision-making ability in the heat of the moment. If more time is what is needed, take it.

I hope you use these tools to better acquaint yourself with the person you are and the person you want to become. As you become more familiar with yourself, you follow the path to finding your life's purpose; it all begins with discovering who you are and what you are made of.

CONSIDERATION #3:
VISION, ACTION, AND RAISING THE BAR

Your visions will become clear only
when you can look into your own heart.
Who looks outside, dreams;
who looks inside, awakes.

—CARL JUNG

I N 1955, A BABY BOY WAS born into a family strongly rooted in the areas of business and politics. In 1973, as a young man, he entered Harvard, and without the slightest clue what he wanted his academic focus to be, he enrolled in pre-law. Although he received good grades, his tenure at the world's most respected university did not last.

The young man took a calculated risk and dropped out of Harvard to devote himself to a vision only he could see. Within a decade, he co-founded a company that became one of the world's most recognized brands, and he became the world's richest man. Of course, the company we are talking about is Microsoft, and the young man was Bill Gates.

In 2002, Gates stated that the mission of Microsoft was "a computer on every desk and in every home." His vision could not have been more clear and concise.

The ability to visualize our goals is utterly essential. Some people may spend decades working toward a goal before the fruits of their labors begin to show. For others, it may take only a few weeks or months. Regardless of how long it takes before you begin to notice results, to achieve any objective it is important to keep moving forward with both sincere desire and a clear vision of what you are working toward.

But what does "vision" mean? The Irish satirist and author of *Gulliver's Travels*, Jonathan Swift, may have defined it best: "Vision is the art of seeing what is invisible to others." I think of vision as a gift that allows you to know, and thus have conviction about, what will be accomplished when there is nothing yet in front of you to prove it.

Take a moment to reflect on what is "real" in your life. Surely there are numerous things you believe to be real that you've never literally seen. Many of us have never seen actual germs, but we still wash our hands before sitting down to eat. We have never seen radiation, but we expect the dentist to put a lead blanket around our throat and chest when he or she X-rays our teeth. Even scientists have never been able to demonstrate under laboratory conditions, and thus empirically prove, the existence of love, yet we all know it exists. When we define our vision by what we deem "possible," we must recognize the potential for unseen "things" to play a role in expanding that definition.

Your vision is a tool of incalculable value. When you learn to focus and refine it, your clear vision can serve as a fuel that propels you to measures beyond anything you have conceived. It is important, therefore, that you work to crystallize your vision so that you can forge this useful tool. Consider that your dreams will forever remain just that—dreams—until you start to make them a reality by first refining them into a vision.

TIMELESS TRUTH: DEFINITIVE PLANNING
AND RESOLUTE ACTION PROMOTE
EXTRAORDINARY RESULTS.

The most efficient approach to crystallizing your vision is through the development and implementation of a plan of action. Author Napoleon Hill characterized the correlation in this way: "First comes thought; then organization of that thought into ideas and plans; then transformation of those plans into reality. The beginning, as you will observe, is in your imagination."

In its simplest form, your action plan (1) outlines your goal, specifically defining what you are after, (2) lists what needs to be done and by whom, (3) gives a time frame during which the plan will be carried out, and (4) identifies the resources required to carry out the plan. Basically, a plan of action lays out your objective and describes how you will get there. If you do not create a clear-cut point of arrival for your journey, no road can take you there. Without an objective and a means of getting there, you will simply wander aimlessly.

In Bill Gates's case, the destination was "a computer on every desk and in every home." In pursuit of that vision, Microsoft now employs more than 90,000 people in more than 100 countries and has managed to get its software on 90 percent of the world's computers.

How did Gates achieve all that? The answer, according to Gates himself, could be paraphrased this way: through the implementation of a plan of action that was derived from an original vision. On the surface, it sounds simple. When you delve deeper into his particular case, you discover the intricacies of Gates's plan and the obstacles Microsoft had to overcome to adhere to his vision.

In the early days of the company, most computers had unique operating systems, systems so unique that the Microsoft research and development team had to create a specialized version of Microsoft's language for each computer on the market.

It required billions of dollars of research, first to establish Microsoft as the standard operating system in the burgeoning personal computer industry and then to stay ahead of the competition. It required the manpower to perform the needed research and the marketing acumen to establish Microsoft in the European and Far Eastern markets. It also required the ability to adapt to a world that was rapidly evolving, sparked by the explosion of digital technology, for much of which Microsoft itself was responsible.

Initially, Microsoft had misunderstood the importance and far-reaching capabilities of the Internet. After gaining some clarity on the untapped potential of the Internet in the mid-1990s, however, Gates steered the company in a new direction that expanded Microsoft's horizons via the World Wide Web as well as into the emerging fields of computer networking, cable television, online magazines, personal digital assistants, video games, Internet telephony, and more. These new directions required an updated vision, and today Microsoft's vision is stated this way: "Create experiences that combine the magic of software with the power of Internet services across a world of devices." This is quite different from Gates's vision of a decade earlier, yet it reflects the company's willingness to adapt to changes brought about, in no small part, by Microsoft itself.

Gates has continued to fine-tune his own vision for an exceptional life. In recent years he has pulled back from active management of Microsoft and devoted more time to worldwide charitable giving. He seems to have taken a page out of the playbook of Scottish-American steel magnate and philanthropist Andrew Carnegie: he has worked to make a fortune, and now he works to give a chunk of it away, to make the world a better place in which to live.

Each of us has the same opportunity as Bill Gates to materialize any idea that we have, to actualize whatever it is we desire, and to create something tangible, profound, and sustainable. That's what the free-enterprise opportunity affords each of us fortunate enough to live in a free society.

However, ideas are like seeds, and not all seeds flourish by themselves. Anyone can plant a seed, and anyone can have a great idea. Even exceptional ideas do not sprout and grow without cultivation. The development of an idea requires a nurturing environment of desire, dedication, and *action*. Ideas without action remain only dreams, always intangible. Consider that it is the people who can intelligently form a plan of action and then faithfully implement their plan who turn their visions into reality.

Ideas are the seeds, but disciplined effort is the water and sunshine that makes them grow.

For You to Consider and Do

The following steps will help you formulate a plan of action to reach your goals.

1. Visualize your goal. Create the clearest possible mental image of your goal. Have a definite point in mind that signifies having attained it, and if necessary, determine the benchmarks that will tell you when you are there. Your goal could be "X amount of dollars in the bank" or "a bachelor of science degree in chemistry" or "my own daily talk show on radio station WXYZ." The more detail, the better.

2. List the steps you will take. Start listing all the steps you know need to be taken to reach your goal. You do not have to put them in order at this stage; just record everything you think needs to occur to bring you to your destination. This list may be very, very

long. In fact, the longer your list is, the better: be as precise as possible about what your journey will entail. Some steps may be conditional, such as, "If accepted for the summer internship at the radio station, revise my summer work schedule." A workable plan of action should have enough flexibility built into it to adapt to the dynamics of life.

3. Start arranging. Go over your list and mark the steps that you know are absolutely paramount to the attainment of your goal. These should become your highest priority. Additionally, you may think of other steps as you sort through your list. Include them. The opposite is also true; you may find items that no longer seem necessary, and you should cross these out.

4. Organize. You are almost there. Give your highest priority steps numbers or letters to signify the order in which they must or should occur. For instance, you must pass a basic chemistry course before you can tackle organic chemistry. Next, slot the smaller steps into the priority list where they are most appropriate. Your plan is taking shape; keep arranging until you have determined the order of all the actions, big and small, that you will take to attain your goal. Put that sequence into a final list, and this will be your action plan. Post it somewhere in plain sight, and make it *big*. You need to read it every day.

5. Review, modify, but most important, *execute*. Begin putting your plan into action, taking the steps in order, and reach the first milestones of your journey. Your action plan will serve as the road map to your destination. If you have done steps 1 through 4 of this exercise well, you will soon find yourself in the driver's seat and on your way toward rewarding results. Review your plan

regularly, and monitor your progress. Update it. If you encounter a roadblock, analyze what you need to do to keep going, then modify your plan accordingly and proceed. Remember that accomplishing all the smaller steps along the way is what will bring you to your big goal.

Consider that the key to step 5 is to focus on the *actions* required to reach your destination rather than the destination itself. If you focus only on the end result, you may miss some steps that are essential to reaching the overarching goal. Your attention to detail as you implement your plan can be the difference between success and failure, so give each step your full effort.

Obviously, what separates a "doer" from a "talker" is action. Successful people take action; they go after what they want with consistent effort and relentless determination. They also know that the interplay between vision and action is dynamic. When you apply consistent effort to a plan of action you have created in order to accomplish your vision, your vision itself becomes further crystallized. Applying this concept carried Bill Gates to greatness. Imagine what it could do for you!

Once you are in the driver's seat and motoring down the road toward your goals, there is a treacherous obstacle you will need to watch out for: an endless stretch of overfamiliar landscape that lulls you into a rut.

TIMELESS TRUTH: WHILE YOU ARE CREATING YOUR FUTURE, COMPLACENCY CAN HALT YOUR PROGRESS.

We shall have no better conditions in the future if we are satisfied with all those which we have at present.
—THOMAS EDISON

Imagine the frequent car trips you take on a route you know well: your daily commute to work, the trip to the supermarket, the route you take to pick up the kids from school. You may have driven the same road for years, perhaps thousands of times. You know every stop sign, every corner, every curve, the blind intersections, the potholes, where you can pass, where you don't dare to pass, and much more. The first few times you drove the route, you were alert. However, as the route became familiar, you settled into a mode close to "autopilot." You may think that your familiar route is the safest one you could possibly take— you know it so well—but the fact is, most car accidents occur close to home. Because of having settled into overfamiliarity, no longer vigilant for anything unforeseen, you may not be ready when something truly unexpected occurs.

The same can happen in a relationship, in your career, or in any part of life where activities have become routine and, therefore, familiar. Familiarity can be a comforting feeling. It is nice to have a job that you know well and to go there each day to receive the wherewithal to live your life. It is wonderful to have a spouse, significant other, or intimate friend with whom you can share your innermost thoughts and feelings day in and day out.

Familiarity, however, can pose a danger to your continuing progress in living a life of significance, and this danger is called complacency. We have all seen sports teams who won a championship one year and appeared poised for similar results the next. However, after an offseason of congratulations, we may see them falter and not even make the playoffs the following year. We have seen the rookie who tears up the league in his first season only to rest on his laurels and struggle mightily the next year. They call it "the sophomore jinx," and it is caused by an attitude of smug satisfaction with one's accomplishments. When we are comfortable in our situation or pleased with our successes, we may forget to apply the process of self-examination necessary for continuous development.

Avoiding the trap of self-satisfaction requires analyzing the past efforts that led to the promotion at work or the league championship or acceptance to the university of one's dreams.

Imagine you have just received the news that you are being promoted to vice president of your firm, with a corner office and a nice raise in pay. After allowing yourself a celebration of some kind, it is already time to take a focused look at what elevated you to this new level. What was it that brought you here—coming in on Saturdays to do paperwork, taking online courses to improve your knowledge about your profession, improving coordination between other departments in the company, a bright marketing idea?

Once you have analyzed what actions and attitudes led to your accomplishments, you will probably want to consider doing more of the same things and, if possible, doing them better. It would behoove you to think about new skill sets that will help you thrive in your new position and exceed normal expectations.

For example, if you have determined that it was your twice-weekly practice sessions at the driving range that enabled you to win the golf tournament, it may be time to add a third session, or at least another bucket of balls. When something good happens in your life, don't rest on your laurels: consider using each success as a springboard to your next victory.

Keep your foot on the gas. Make the effort to understand and internalize what you have accomplished and what it took to get you there. Self-satisfaction and complacency are vanquished most effectively by an attitude of determination to raise the bar in whatever we do.

TIMELESS TRUTH: CONSISTENT EFFORTS YIELD SUPERLATIVE GROWTH.

Albert Einstein once offered the opinion that one should not set personal goals that are easily achievable; rather, one should set goals that are barely achievable through one's greatest efforts. Whether you are one who strives for grandiosity or whether a life of simplicity is what you desire, raising the bar is necessary for you to fully realize your ideal lifestyle, whatever that may be.

Apple's Steve Jobs was legendary for raising the bar. The creative head at Pixar Studios once said that Jobs understood the potential of computer-animated films even before the studio's writers and artists did. At Apple, Jobs continually demanded that the bar be raised and had faith that his engineering and design teams could reach his standards. In fact, he routinely demanded they do so.

> One day, in a meeting with the engineers who created the iPod, Steve Jobs was presented with the latest prototype. He held the prototype in his hands, played with it, then rejected it on the basis that it was simply too big. The engineers countered that it could not be made smaller, and that with this iPod they had already raised the bar for electronics design by several quantum leaps. Jobs listened quietly to their argument, and then he stood up, walked over to an aquarium in the office, and dropped the prototype into the tank. As it sank, bubbles floated up from the bottom. The air bubbles, Jobs told his engineers, meant that there had been air in the device, and therefore, there was also space that could be eliminated. The engineers got the point and, because they had no choice but to excel, they found a way to make the device smaller.

Everyone who becomes great, in whatever field, works for it. Therefore, ask yourself: do I want to become better at what I do? Not many would say no to such a question. Most engineers would say they would like to be a better engineer, most doctors would like to be a better doctor, and so on. Do you desire to become the first-rate version of yourself? If so, the question is whether or not you are willing to put in the work required for such gain.

Taking "baby steps" is a practical approach to achieving those lofty, long-term goals that Einstein prescribed. An incremental approach certainly worked for the well-known inventor Thomas Edison, who dedicated himself to smaller goals—many, many experiments—in his quest to produce many world-changing inventions, including the electrical storage battery.

It is said that Edison failed fifty thousand times in his effort to create a workable battery for storing electricity. As the story goes, when someone remarked on his lack of results from his huge number of failed experiments, Edison replied, "I have gotten lots of results. I know fifty thousand things that won't work." Each one of the unsuccessful experiments was, in fact, a baby step toward success, and making the attempt fifty thousand times certainly meets Albert Einstein's criterion of "one's greatest efforts."

Similarly, in the process that led to the incandescent light bulb, Edison tried many different types of filaments before finding one that burned long enough to make his bulb commercially viable. The motion picture camera, the phonograph, and numerous others of the 1,300 inventions for which he receives credit went through similar processes of incremental success before arriving at a major achievement. Today, no other man has had a broader or more lasting impact on the daily lives of people around the world than has Thomas Edison through his inventions, the results of many small efforts.

Setting short-term objectives—goals that are more easily attainable—fosters your individual confidence, strengthens your resolve, and cements the belief that *all* your goals are attainable. This works to raise the bar incrementally once each goal is met. Consider holding yourself to a high standard. Demand the absolute best from yourself, as Einstein advised, and *do it daily*. The very act of raising the bar will keep you from falling into the quicksand of complacency, while consistently achieving short-term goals will promote continuous and superlative growth.

Without first reaching your initial objectives, or interim goals, and thus establishing a new level to work from, the next level may seem more difficult to achieve. Imagine a cleaning crew washing the windows on a Manhattan skyscraper. Visualize how difficult it would be for them to clean the windows of the story above without raising the staging platform they stand on. Rather than trying to stretch for something that is out of reach, it clearly makes more sense to finish one level at a time, then raise the platform and continue to work from a higher level.

Try to incorporate small, measurable objectives, or baby steps, into your journey toward your dreams. When you complete an individual goal, raise your platform, and move to the next level and the next set of tasks.

Remember that your ability to continually "raise the bar" is essential, not only for your growth and progress, but also so you can continually reevaluate your potential. Can you imagine never challenging yourself? How would you ever strengthen your weaknesses? Most likely, you would not. Building a life replete with value and significance hinges on your ability to be proactive and honestly face your weaknesses (raise the bar) and to set and attain short-term goals to correct them (take baby steps), as well as on your ability to create a new level for yourself to work on (raise the platform).

If our achievements and those of others have taught us anything, it is that great things are rarely achievable without great effort. It is only practical, then, to believe that a person will not distinguish him- or herself from others without working diligently. It may appear to the public eye that certain individuals have "built Rome in a day," but almost without exception, there was much blood, sweat, and tears out of view that was part of a long period of many smaller efforts.

I challenge you to challenge yourself: identify the levels of achievement you desire, and then actively pursue them. We must truly desire meaning in our lives to eventually achieve it. You have something within you to offer this world that will make it a better place—each one of us does. Consider that you owe it to yourself and others to pursue your full potential.

Dale Carnegie once said, "The world is full of people who are grabbing and self-seeking. So the rare individual who unselfishly tries to serve others has an enormous advantage. He has little competition." Carnegie also quoted Owen D. Young, a successful American businessman and diplomat, who said, "People who can put themselves in the place of other people, who can understand the workings of their minds, need never worry about what the future has in store for them."

Consider these comments as you interact with others. They allude to depths of your potential, which become illuminated when you passionately strive to better not only yourself but the people around you. When you raise the bar for yourself, the potential of those around you naturally tends to rise as well. Take a moment to ask yourself what you and those around you are capable of achieving. It's worth asking: How great do you believe you could become at what you do? What could you attain? How much change can you potentially create, and how many lives could you touch? What effect will you have on this world, and what kind of legacy will you imprint? How many smiles will you have placed on the faces of others? How much can you do with the time you have?

The world needs you to share your strengths; consider applying your efforts diligently and consistently so you can contribute the full extent of your potential. And consider doing so without strings attached. As Carnegie and Young promised, life will pay you back.

For You to Consider and Do

The following exercise will help you to "raise the bar":

1. Determine the areas of your life where you want to operate at a higher level: Work? School? Family? Personal relationships? Your hobby?

2. On your computer or in your journal, describe how you would like each area to look in six months or one year from now.

3. Next, isolate what would have to change over that time span for your goal to become a reality. Would you have to respond to events in a different way? Would you have to accomplish more in less time? Would the quality of your approach need to improve? Think this through and record your answers for all areas. Where the changes involve taking specific steps, record the steps in sequence and establish a time frame for them.

4. Whatever necessary changes you have identified, know that these changes are the means to promoting a better and happier you. As Don Hutson says, it is a blessing to have a willingness within you to change that is stronger than your devotion to old habits.

5. Make the conscious decision to raise the bar. Begin implementing the steps and changes you recorded in step 3, and do so at your very next opportunity. Without your follow-

through, nothing will happen. You've already admitted that you want to raise the bar; with your dedication, it *will* happen.

6. At regular intervals, review your list and evaluate your progress. If you have shared your desire to raise the bar with a confidante, go ahead and ask how he or she believes you are progressing. You may find that baby steps soon lead to giant strides in the right direction. What was once outside your comfort zone may now be routine, and as a result, you will know you are closer to your goals.

I challenge you to raise the bar in your life. Push yourself to take on that next set of goals and that new set of tasks, and then methodically work your way through, level by level. Be mindful of your choices, actions, and habits, and determine whether they are assisting you in your efforts. You have the ability to accomplish much more than you have ever anticipated—we all do. As individuals, we simply cannot comprehend our potential until we tap into it.

May you consistently and honorably raise the bar, in your own life and in the lives of others, and by doing so, may you fill your cup and drink from the saucer.

CONSIDERATION #4:
THE SCALE OF LIFE:
FINDING BALANCE, RELEASING THE POWER OF APPRECIATION, AND LEARNING FROM THE EXPERIENCE OF OTHERS

Be thankful for what you have; you'll end up having more. If you concentrate on what you don't have, you will never, ever have enough.
—OPRAH WINFREY

TIMELESS TRUTH: BALANCE IS ESSENTIAL.

LIKEN YOUR LIFE TO THE raising of a majestic skyscraper. Similarly, compare your life to a train's course along which it remains focused and on track. Think of the things that carry you through life's anxieties, and from problems to their solutions, as sturdy bridges. These analogies have something in common: steel. The mark of modern industrial society is the many different types of steel in almost limitless applications. From an automobile chassis to surgical tools, from building girders to the watch on your wrist, steel is everywhere.

Steel is mostly iron mixed with smaller amounts of other metals depending on the desired application. The correct ratio of the raw materials is critical to producing a material that will withstand the stresses and strains to which it will be subjected. If the balance is not exact, the resulting metal may bend, weaken, corrode, or rust, and fail to fulfill the purpose for which it was forged. However, if the proper amounts of carbon, nickel, chromium, manganese, and/or other metals

75

are incorporated during the steel-making process, the result is a scalpel sharp enough for a surgeon's use, a drill hard enough to bore through rock, a girder burly enough to span a river, or sheet metal corrosive-resistant enough for a kitchen sink.

In all cases, the ingredients have to be combined in the right balance to reach the intended purpose. The same is true of the components of your life. The raw materials of your existence are the contents of your mind—including your attitudes, emotions, thoughts, intentions, and dreams—and your physical self. From these raw materials you can build the most magnificent creations during your time on the earth, provided that the ingredients are properly combined in the crucible of your own life—in other words, if you are living a life of balance.

A properly balanced life keeps you focused and on track, aimed at your destination. Having balance can carry you over the anxieties that bubble up in everyday life. Perhaps most important, balance adds structural integrity to the motivating forces—your will and desire—that propel your success.

> Finding a balance between my professional life and personal life was, for a time, one of the biggest challenges I experienced after entering the business world. For as long as I can remember, I have always had a craving for achievement and a competitive heart. However, my approach to the journey, and my understanding of what success truly is, has evolved. In my teens, I would wake up and jump out of bed, thinking that time spent sleeping was time wasted. I would rush to get ready, sometimes missing breakfast. I would rush out the door, often without saying so much as "Have a good day" to my mother.
>
> I was missing some of the "smaller," yet actually more important, things in life. At the time, my focus was on how much work I could get done in one day. After a few people

"kindly" pointed out this characteristic of my personality, I could see that I needed to slow down a bit and modify the way I approached life. Paradoxically, since slowing down a bit, the number of things that I have been able to accomplish in a day has *increased*.

When I wake up in the morning, I still jump out of bed. I am excited simply to be alive. Life is the ultimate gift. However, I sleep more than I used to, and—because I am better rested—I am more efficient. I am able to think more clearly and therefore to accomplish more in a shorter time frame. It has been said many times that breakfast is the most important meal of the day. It is the fuel that gets me going, and I now eat breakfast every day before I leave the house. Whenever I take leave of the members of my family, I take time to let them know how much they are appreciated.

Some of the adjustments I made may sound inconsequential, but the benefits of bringing balance to one's life are universal and self-evident, and greater than you'd think. Taking better care of oneself, spending more time with friends and family, and—strange as it may seem—at the same time accomplishing more work in a day, making more money, and playing more are all hallmarks of a life of balance.

Creating balance is essential, and it is a key component to the success of any person's routine. The difficult task is *maintaining* this balance once you find it.

We have all heard that eating right and exercising regularly is the key to a healthy body. We know that we need a certain amount of calories and grams of protein, fats, and carbohydrates per day to maintain nutritional balance, and that some nutritional elements are in higher demand by our bodies than others. The same is true of the elements that nurture our minds and make us efficient at whatever we are doing.

Indeed, we know that much more than diet and exercise is required for a healthy lifestyle. Friends, happiness, laughter, true passion, love, a sense of belonging, hobbies, and day-to-day activities all play a significant role in our overall well-being. Relationships with friends and family, hobbies, work, exercise—attaining a well-balanced blend of these things can bring you a satisfying level of happiness. Not everyone needs or wants a big house or fancy car, but everyone you've ever met inherently strives for happiness in one form or another. Arguably, happiness is the most universal form of wealth.

You can position yourself to receive all of the great gifts life has to offer by making sure to give yourself ample and appropriate time for each and every component of a balanced life, each and every day. If followed closely, this simple regimen will bring you benefits sooner than you may expect. Positive changes will begin to crop up in your life, seemingly out of nowhere.

However, the same is true of negative effects: they will continue to crop up where there is a lack of balance. Nutritionists give this example: If you eat a meal high in calories but nutritionally empty, you probably will not feel a difference tomorrow. And if you eat this type of food at every meal for a week, you still may not notice a significant difference. However, over the course of a month or longer, you will start to see and feel the results of a month's unhealthy choices. It was not the last burger you ate or the last box of fries for lunch that brought about your decreased energy level and physical condition. Rather, it was the full month of consistently unbalanced nutrition.

How you handle exercise, meals, hobbies, friendships, relationships, work, and family affects both you in the now and the person you are becoming. The not-so-little things in life have much to offer, so make an honest attempt each day to create and maintain a solid balance in all areas of your life. Most of all, remember that a fine balance of the right components will bring you significant results in all arenas, including some unexpected bonuses.

For You to Consider and Do

To attain balance in your life, consider a plan that works in reverse.

1. First, ask yourself what combination of things you would like in your life. For example, do you want to spend time at work, with friends, with family, exercising, in the outdoors, cooking or baking, exploring restaurants in your region, taking yoga classes, playing a sport, watching movies or television, relaxing at the ocean, and so on?

2. Write down these components of your life (work, social life, time with family, exercise, etc.) on a sheet of paper. Now, consider the relative amount of time you want to spend on each. Also, establish in your mind that you are your own watchdog, the person who will make sure you bring balance to your own life. Nobody else will do it for you—nor should they.

3. Compartmentalize your week. There are only 168 hours to spend; the question is, exactly how are you going to spend them? Of course, a large portion is taken by the recommended 8 hours of sleep per night: that's 56 hours of your week (and it's nonnegotiable—adequate sleep is crucial to maintaining both your physical health and mental equanimity). Also, let's assume that an average of 40 hours per week are spent working—you're up to 96 hours of your weekly allotment. So, how are you going to spend your remaining 72?

4. Assign priority to the things that deserve more of your time, such as family and exercise. Allocate the number of hours per day or per week that you can spend on each, based on your preference, but also remembering that you only have 72 hours to spend. Be sure to give ample time to each item that you list. Remember, the objective of this exercise is to create balance, not chaos.

5. Next, begin to carve out time each day for the items that bring additional balance to your life. This can be a challenging step, but you must hold yourself accountable for doing each of the listed items each day, or as often as you determined in your calculations. Again, you are the watchdog.

There will be days when you are tempted to say, "I just don't have the time." This expression demonstrates why some people do not have balance in their lives. We somehow find a way to make ourselves "so busy" that we just can't seem to do what we know we ought to do. Of course, that is exactly the reason for this exercise. If you have to, force yourself to commit to the times allotted every day. Once you begin to see the fruits of your efforts, such as less stress and increased happiness, it will become easier to carve out the hours you need. We are creatures of habit, and your newly designed routine will soon seem normal. In time, it will become a routine you wouldn't think of changing.

6. Finally, monitor your plan for implementing balance in your life. Keep track of how you spend your time and how much time you actually dedicate to each item listed, and write it all down. When you literally see how you use your time, you can then identify the areas of your life that need more and less of your time and attention.

This new approach will eventually become your routine. Before you know it, balance will creep into your life in a way that leaves you feeling more fulfilled and accomplished.

TIMELESS TRUTH: APPRECIATING ALL YOU HAVE INCREASES YOUR ABILITY TO ATTAIN EVEN MORE.

Without balance, the stresses, pressures, and anxieties that accumulate from living a life out of whack can have a negative impact on one of your most important tools, a tool anyone can employ for attaining significance in life: the power of appreciation.

My long-time friend, mentor, and associate Brian Heath says, "If you're not grateful for what you have, you will never be happy with what you want!" Certainly we have all been guilty of accepting a gift that life has offered while simultaneously turning to look for more, not fully acknowledging or appreciating the value of what we were given.

Growing up with a sense that something was lacking, Brian worked hard to create a life to which many would aspire: a wonderful family with two lovely daughters and the material trappings of success. By all accounts, he was happy and successful. Yet Brian had always been driven more by getting than giving, and this mind-set became more fixed as his life progressed. A sense that something was missing blinded him to the value of certain things he already had.

Later, Brian would liken his old attitude to that of an art enthusiast who bought a Picasso and hung it on the wall and, for a time, delighted in it. In the weeks or months that followed, though, the man passed by his Picasso and barely noticed, much less appreciated, the miracle of artistic creation that graced his home. That was what Brian's life had become, but he didn't realize it until the day his wife said she was divorcing him.

What ensued was extreme emotional pain as Brian lost "his Picasso," the treasure he had forgotten he had. Fortunately, this pain brought Brian to the life-changing realization that the only real lack he had experienced in his entire life was a lack of gratitude. After that, Brian's beliefs did not change so much as his awareness did: now he strives to notice and appreciate all that he has—his family and friends, his job and his clients, his health and his financial security, and his many other blessings. (Brian has graciously allowed me to include in this book his essay "My Picasso," which tells the full story of his transformation. You can find it in the appendix on page 185.)

We sometimes take for granted certain things, opportunities, and relationships in our lives, even if the effects haven't yet been as corrosive as those Brian suffered. Regardless of our situation, in life we all have it much better than we believe we do. In fact, if we had nothing beyond the simple blessing of the gift of life, that would be enough. However, there is so much more.

For You to Consider and Do

1. Take a moment to visualize yourself as you first wake up in the morning: What is your routine? You probably wash yourself, dry off, and get dressed. You eat breakfast. What else? You may simply hasten your way to your car and drive to work. Consider for a moment: Did you stop to notice how fortunate you are? Did you consider the physical and mental capabilities with which you have been blessed?

2. Now let's recast your morning routine from an appreciative mind-set: You wake up, open your eyes, and rise out of bed. Your mind is working. You notice you are fully cognizant of what you are going to do today. You walk to the shower. You see your motor skills are functioning perfectly. You shower, towel off, and get dressed. You are grateful for the hot water at your fingertips. You can see where your clothes are, and you can discern which clothes match and which do not. You have been blessed with the gift of sight to see the beauty in this world.

You go to the kitchen to eat breakfast. You can enjoy the delicious flavors of this world: you smell the aroma of your freshly brewed coffee, feel the texture of the crispy toast, and taste the succulence of fresh strawberries. As you drive down the road, you experience your hand-eye coordination, and you feel grateful for the speed of your car and the convenience it affords you. You are so aware that, if necessary, you could react to what is going on around you in milliseconds. How does this morning feel different from the first one?

Some people want more out of life than others, and this is not a bad thing. Actually, it is wonderful, especially if the desire for more drives them to bring value to their lives and to the lives of others. When we are introduced to our individual gifts and blessings, it is for a reason: to use them with the sincere intent to benefit both ourselves and everyone else.

If you take a few moments to reflect, every innovation and every amenity we take for granted today is the result of some other individual's desire for "more" at some time in the past. Just look around: modern high-efficiency homes, better cars, healthier foods, advanced medicines—all these creations reflect the genius of the human mind. If you stop to see these gifts with fresh eyes, you will gain a deeper appreciation for how much the work of so many others has brought you.

This mental shift will change the way you view the world. Your ability to be appreciative of what you have is like wearing a pair of glasses that magnifies everything you see, do, have, and touch. Consider approaching everything you have, every privilege you enjoy, every friendly person and sunny day, with an attitude of enjoyment and gratitude, and each becomes an amazing gift life has to offer.

Your appreciative mind-set will impact you to the core. It will make you happier and more content, more aware of all you currently have. Your appreciation of all you have will put any negative feelings you experience into perspective, and it will deflate the power of your daily anxieties and stresses. Gratitude will allow you to charge forward in life with a much clearer mind-set and more precise ideas about what you have and, therefore, what you want to achieve. It will give you the positive outlook you need to carry your plans through.

A sense of appreciation and gratitude also affects the way you look at others, and therefore it strongly influences the way you talk to them and treat them and, most important, how you make them feel. Positive attitudes are magnetic. You will soon find yourself possessing an attitude that people naturally gravitate toward, and you will begin to see yourself as someone who is able to bring the strengths of others to the surface and help people to see the gifts they have to offer. Inevitably, you will change the way people feel with your positive energy, which is rooted in your positive outlook on life.

With a little effort, maintaining a consistently positive mental attitude can become a natural way of life. Consider that your decision to consciously implement an appreciative outlook will influence those around you to be more appreciative as well. As you model an attitude of appreciation, people around you will begin to notice the simpler gifts that life has to offer. They too will start to view their relatively luxurious possessions in a different light. They too may walk out their front door tomorrow and really appreciate that new car, or fully realize how fortunate they are to have nice clothes to wear, food in their cupboards, and a roof over their head at night. Not all people in this world are blessed with such gifts.

Consider that appreciation is a key motivator in attempting to promote positive changes in the world. Perhaps if we were all to realize how much we have, we would become more inclined to help those who are less fortunate. A glance at the abundance in our own lives with an appreciative eye often inspires us to become more selfless and to help others, and in this way practicing appreciation is also our responsibility.

The lesson here is to begin actively appreciating what you have at this very moment. You may find that at this moment you don't have exactly what you want in life; that's OK. You may not have Donald Trump's property, Warren Buffett's net worth, or Bill Gates's company, but if you earnestly visualize your life and everything in it, you will quickly discover many things for which to be eternally grateful. You will see the Picassos.

Step outside, take a breath of air, and smell its freshness. You are blessed. Taste that chocolate bar. Stop and listen—what do you hear? Do you hear birds singing, children laughing, or the sounds of music in your home? Congratulations. You are blessed with the gifts of taste and hearing. Take a moment to hug a loved one and feel their affection. Again, you are fortunate and blessed. In so many ways, we all are. Now allow yourself to bathe in the end result of all this appreciation: pure, genuine happiness.

Most people living lives of true significance have discovered for themselves that the material items that people acquire over the course of their lives, those physical items that many of us believe make us happy, are minor pieces of a larger picture. One's character, relationships, value to others, and most cherished personal memories are far more important pieces of the picture. If you have worked diligently, when all the pieces are assembled, the picture you will have created will reflect the level of happiness you attracted into your life.

Recent studies point up definite correlations between our happiness and our degree of appreciation or gratitude. In a 2003 study, scientists Robert Emmons and Michael McCullough concluded that the simple practice of expressing gratitude each day increased levels of happiness in the study's subjects by an astounding 25 percent.

> Subjects of the experiment were divided into three groups. Each week, one group wrote down five things they were grateful for during the week. The next group wrote down five things that had been a distraction in their daily lives, and the third group simply wrote down five events that happened, without regard to whether each was positive or negative. At the end of ten weeks, the group that practiced gratitude was found to be 25 percent happier than the control group who listed five events of any kind.

Other studies have demonstrated that practicing gratitude as little as once per week has a positive effect on levels of happiness. If something so simple as appreciating what you already have can lead to such a profound effect on your overall happiness, shouldn't you strongly consider incorporating gratitude into your daily routine?

For You to Consider and Do

You can do this simple exercise daily or weekly. It takes only a minute or two, but it can have big effects. Consider following these steps to improve your mood, your level of happiness, and your positive impact.

1. Think of three things that you are grateful for, that is, three things that benefit you and that make your life better.

2. Now, think about the source of each of these three things: how has each come to be in your life?

3. Tomorrow or next week and every day or week to follow, think about three more things that you truly appreciate having in your life. These can be different aspects of the things you listed before or different things altogether.

4. Think about the reasons why these thi_ _ are in your life.

That is all there is to it. As you w _ _now, thinking about something negative such as an o_ _ _ _ _ll or an argument will deflate your mood. T_ _ _ _ _ _ _ _ is true as well. A positive, appreciative th_ _ _ _ _ _ elevate your mood just as easily. Consider maki _ _ _tude a h_b_t, and watch for the results.

As you can see, each of us has much for which to be grateful. Keep in mind that life can change at any moment, and the gifts we have are not necessarily ours to keep forever. Life has a peculiar tendency to throw us curveballs at times we least expect them, which is all the more reason to be alert in every moment to the gifts at hand. Consider that gratitude will generate a positive outlook that can bring you happiness resiliency, inspire those around you, and give you both the strength o go after what you desire and the inclination to be of benefit to others. It is my hope you appreciate all that you have and therefore open yourself t_ _ receiving even more.

TIMELESS TRUTH: WHILE YOU ARE BUSY
MAINTAINING BALANCE AND APPRECIATING
ALL YOU HAVE, LIFE WILL NEVERTHELESS BRING
UNWELCOME EVENTS. REGARDLESS, GRATITUDE
MUST REMAIN THE FOUNDATION OF
YOUR ATTITUDE.

How we react to these curveballs determines the wisdom we gain from life's unforeseen events. At the most unexpected of times, situations will arise that put their mark on us, leaving us forever changed. The story that follows comes from a man I greatly admire named Ken. I met Ken in a professional context a couple years back and have enjoyed my time and conversations with him ever since. His story imparts the message that any of life's experiences, even the tragic ones, have the potential to convey wisdom and promote personal growth. I am indebted to him for sharing his story here. I hope it leaves a positive impression on you, as it certainly did on me.

Ken's Story

In March 2008 I had been divorced for nearly six years, and all of my children had since moved away. I was living in two separate locations and working out of town. My father had recently become nonambulatory and nonverbal with dementia and was in a local nursing home. I had his power of attorney and was his primary contact with the outside world.

My job was exciting, as it had always been, challenging and with constant responsibility. However, the conclusion to this successful career was on the near horizon. Approaching retirement, I had no significant other and spent much of my free time walking, biking, and skiing to stay fit.

Amidst all of this, I started to experience a sudden acute

pain in my right knee. My primary care physician sent me in for an MRI, and the results were certainly unexpected. Soft-tissue tumors in and behind my knee joint were found. The tumors had surely been growing for some time, as they were now invading my proximal tibia and my calf muscle.

The next day, a thoracic scan showed multiple lung lesions and liver cysts. Next, a whole-body bone scan displayed five "hot spots," three of which were of known etiology (cause), but others were still unexplained after further X-rays.

All these lesions were described by the radiologist as "compatible with metastatic foci with a malignant tumor." Orthopedic surgeons explained to me that this tumor type was very rare (one case per million). I was then told that the tumors could be either benign or malignant. Scared beyond belief, I was advised against biopsy and told I should be at Massachusetts General Hospital in Boston the next day. So I was.

My first day at MGH, I spent four hours at the office and in the lab visiting with the oncology team, and was soon scheduled for surgery. The surgeons told me that the tumors would undergo a biopsy during the surgery. If the results were benign, the tumors still might recur down the road with a slight chance of becoming malignant. If the tumors were found to be malignant, they would amputate my leg immediately. If this happened, the game plan was for me to go home to take time to heal, then get a prosthetic and probably live between one and two more years. I was sent to visit the local Hanger Prosthetics office prior to my surgery so that I could become more informed about what may be in store.

The people at Hanger Prosthetics were great about educating me and gave me tips for the surgery, but at the same time, the visit really heightened my fear. I had to say good-bye to Dad, not knowing if he understood what was really happening, and had to arrange for a new power of attorney and alternate contacts for Dad. I said good-bye to my three best woman friends and my coworkers. I was scared beyond belief.

I rode to MGH in Boston with my daughter. I had spoken with my two boys by phone the night before the surgery, only to find out when I got there that they were waiting at the hospital for my daughter and me. This blew me away. This was a surreal moment. Everyone at the hospital was supportive, and my kids were with me until the last minute right outside the surgery room, as well as the moment I woke up.

There were four surgeons, two anesthesiologists, and four nurses/techs in the surgery room. I woke up in the recovery room thinking I was in another realm or world, but at the end of my bed I could see two feet sticking up, which I needed to have confirmed by one of the surgeons.

"It was benign, Doc!" I exclaimed.

Physical therapy started the next morning, and I was released two days after surgery. I walked two miles just five days after surgery, and I never looked back. Tumor remnants were still present one month after surgery, but I am still symptom-free thirty-four months later.

It took me nearly six months of sick leave to recover, due to complications from the surgery. I had to have a repair on an inguinal hernia just three months after the knee surgery and an emergency appendectomy two weeks after that. After these complications were addressed, though, I was mentally back in the game. I hiked my first two mountains ten and eleven weeks after the knee surgery. I continued hiking

Maine's mountains just two weeks after the third surgery (the appendectomy), and I had hiked thirty-one mountains and skied four days by year's end. My dad died just before Christmas in 2008, and I retired ten days later, eight and a half months after the tumor surgery. I saw that life was too short. I needed more time to simply live life.

Since then, I've continued walking four miles per day, hiking thirty-five to forty mountains per year, skiing eighteen to twenty-eight days per year, biking, gardening, and traveling around the country to see my favorite music artists in concert. I also built myself a new, small, energy-efficient house in which to live out the rest of my life. I don't know what my future holds, but I take life a day at a time, try to stay in touch with my children and friends, stay active, and continue working on introspection and my spiritual evolution through daily meditation and an appreciation of the beauty of nature's treasures around me.

Ken's story illuminates the importance of the small-seeming but more important things in life, the things that possess true weight. It is not that Ken did not appreciate his blessings before his life-altering experience, but rather that now he views life from a different angle. He came to understand deeply how short life truly is, and simultaneously, he was able to experience the depths of love by having his family there at his bedside during his time of physical and emotional need.

Ken can now look out from a mountaintop and know that, if his leg had been amputated, those landscapes would have gone unseen. Before his surgery, as he wondered how his day-to-day capabilities would be affected if his leg were amputated, his retirement and the activities with which he wanted to fill his retirement years flashed before his eyes. Without that big scare, Ken would not have gained the benefit of a clear perspective on his own life.

There is much to learn from the life-altering experiences of other people. Hearing their stories can highlight the miracles each of us has in our own lives and help us to appreciate the gifts that are already there. In effect, the inspirational stories of others can help us live in such a way that the person we *are* and the person we are *becoming* is someone who understands how to live a life filled with things that celebrate life itself.

The take-home message from Ken's story is profound. All life's experiences will mold you into the person you become, influence the ways in which you think, and affect the goals you set for yourself. Sometimes, we will be unprepared for what life has in store for us. However, the wisdom that we gain from such situations can genuinely augment the quality of our lives and the lives of others.

No matter what you do, climb all the mountains, take in all the landscapes, and pack your future with all you want it to include. May it be abundant with happiness, and may you appreciate all that you have.

CONSIDERATION #5:
SUCCESS IS NOT A DESTINATION,
IT IS A JOURNEY

Success is getting what you want, happiness is wanting what you get.
—DAVE GARDNER

TIMELESS TRUTH: THERE IS MORE TO
SUCCESS THAN SUCCESS ITSELF.

THE STORY GOES THAT SOMEONE once asked the Dalai Lama what surprises him most. "Man," he replied, "because he sacrifices his health in order to make money. Then he sacrifices his money to recuperate his health. And then he is so anxious about the future that he does not enjoy the present; the result being that he does not live in the present or the future; he lives as if he is never going to die, and then dies never having really lived." Words of truth.

While climbing to the mountaintops of life, don't forget, as the saying goes, to "stop and smell the roses." A life of value and meaning obviously includes the journey itself, meaning all of the people met and the friendships formed, the places visited and memories made, the lessons learned and the wisdom shared, as well as the material possessions accumulated.

The success associated with genuine significance could be characterized as everything you experience between the time you crystallize your vision and when you reach the end result. The "in-between" is what most deeply affects the person you become and the memories you will forever call your own. Once you have begun your journey, consider gathering as many experiences as you can to store in your memory vault and to draw from in the future.

As we discussed in Consideration 4, balance is one factor that helps ensure you'll have a full, readily available stash of memories and diverse experiences. You can attain such balance by participating in the things you love, such as activities with family and friends. It could be anything, really: fishing, boating, mountain climbing, exercising, reading, doing puzzles, walking, volunteering, hobbies, reading, spending time with your kids...whatever makes you happy.

Each activity serves as a form of self-improvement. Doing what you truly enjoy helps create a strong and healthy outlook. Doing what you care for promotes happiness, helps clear your mind, and keeps you on track. In fact, research studies have demonstrated that time invested in activities that engage your mind and add balance to your life make you more productive and creative in other areas of your life as well.

On the contrary, there are countless examples of those who have set out on a track for success and then never looked back. They never changed gears, never slowed down to enjoy what they had created, and then, all of a sudden, they reached the end of the road. They accomplished everything they had wanted to but never truly experienced the ride.

Not taking notice of the gems along the way can lead to what is often called "the success trap." Some people attain the material trappings of success, yet they neglect to strive for balance. The pressures of coping with their push toward "success" have led millions of people to use antidepressants, alcohol, drugs, tranquilizers, painkillers, and other quick fixes in search of the relaxation and happiness they crave instead of understanding the root of their problem. Then there is the toll the success trap takes on one's health in the form of ulcers, cardiovascular disease, and cancers. With all this in mind, remember the words of the Dalai Lama.

People often create rationalizations for the trap they find themselves in. A common one is, "I will keep at it until I truly make it." I once met an extremely wealthy man who had worked like a dog to accumulate more than $700 million. Once he had achieved that, he vowed not to back off until he reaches $1 billion. At the time, his daughters were growing up, and never once had he attended one of their tennis tournaments. This man was in the success trap then, he is in it now, and his mind-set ensures that he will stay there. Some would describe this approach to life as tragic.

There is a critical difference between *accomplishing* and *experiencing your accomplishments*. The difference explains why some people feel empty after their journey is over. Remember, it is during the journey that success truly manifests itself.

Another common belief of those in the success trap is, "I am how much I make." Such a distortion ignores the many gifts each of us has to give as well as the many other aspects of life essential for happiness. This limited attitude prevents one from finding the balance that leads to true fulfillment.

Then we find people who say, "Once I'm successful, then I will slow down and bring balance to my life." Unfortunately, all too often that particular success never comes, and so the time of enjoying life remains parked in a distant, intangible future. Even when such people do accomplish their goals, they may immediately reset them, continually putting off enjoying their achievements and their blessings. We could imagine that our friend working toward his $1 billion will have a truly rich life once he has reached his goal. However, like many, he may misinterpret his feelings of general dissatisfaction as evidence that he doesn't yet have enough material success.

The success trap generates another phenomenon that can bring a life of significance and happiness to a rapid halt: burnout. The hallmark of burnout is long-term physical and emotional exhaustion coupled with the feeling that the rewards gained have been inadequate. Burnout may lead not only to disinterest in one's work but also to inferior performance and even poorer health. The habit of working harder and longer while neglecting one's needs and health will sooner or later decrease one's enjoyment of one's work and, eventually, one's personal relationships. If carried on too long, this approach can lead to physical and emotional collapse.

It is difficult to articulate the importance of truly experiencing your accomplishments, but this is clear: we must make the time to slow down and enjoy the fruits of our labors.

Consider challenging yourself to taste the fruits of your labors. Take time to experience what you have accomplished. It will empower you. Take time to consider the value your accomplishments bring to your life and to the other people in it: family, friends, and strangers alike. This will make you better at what you do, more focused on what holds true weight, and therefore, more able and likely to meet your next set of goals. Enjoying your successes can serve as a powerful motivator. Allow yourself to use this advice as a tool to move forward, to accomplish, and most important, to experience it all.

TIMELESS TRUTH: THE JOURNEY IS ABOUT FINDING HAPPINESS.

I recall hearing one time about a fabulously successful woman, a self-made millionaire who, by all accounts, had enough wealth to live in luxury for lifetimes. She advised global hedge funds, recruited top talent for financial institutions, and was instrumental in developing strategies for top firms in the financial services industry. In short, she was supremely competent at what she did and very well rewarded for her work. She enjoyed considerable material benefits as a result of her success and had not even reached her prime. Her victories were anything but small. Then she contracted breast cancer.

During her ordeal, she underwent a profound spiritual transformation, after which closing million-dollar deals no longer provided the same thrill it once had. No longer did the material symbols of her success hold as much meaning. She realized that none of those objects had showed up to visit her in the hospital, but people who were important to her, and to whom she was important, did show up to spend time at her bedside. They came to tell her how much she meant to them, and how much they loved her.

Her cancer was cured, and now she often comments that breast cancer was the best thing that ever happened to her. It opened her eyes and her heart to the things in life that are so much more important than diamond necklaces or fancy automobiles, a side of life that had been hidden behind a heavy curtain of wealth and work. Today, she is an activist for breast cancer research, works to raise awareness of the deep inequities of our nation's health care system, and engages in philanthropic causes.

The challenge of her illness helped this millionaire gain a profound appreciation for the aspects of life that resonate more deeply than material possessions—things such as friendship, love, kindness, compassion, and gratitude. In truth, these are the same elements that bring the gift of enduring happiness, regardless of material wealth.

When I was younger, I perceived success as something measured in dollars or material objects such as homes, cars, or boats— things accumulated by this woman and by my mentor Philip (see Consideration 1). Although my lack of understanding about success could have be attributed to my youth or limited life experience, nonetheless I have since met numerous individuals who make millions of dollars per year and suffer under the same delusion. They have beautiful homes, drive magnificent automobiles, vacation at exotic destinations multiple times per year, and wear expensive clothing, and they have something else in common.

Despite all the "razzle-dazzle," I have observed that many of these multimillionaires lack genuine happiness. At first, I was puzzled when I met people who seemed to have it all and yet were obviously unfulfilled. I wondered how this was possible. Eventually it became clear that they were actually lacking quite a lot.

Although some people have material wealth, they may not have the items of life that possess true weight, or the items of significance that lead to lasting fulfillment. If they do have these things, they simply may not notice them. For them these things have become what my friend Brian Heath would refer to as a "Picasso."

It is no secret that most people are in search of significance in their lives in some way. Naturally, finding this significance or meaning is accompanied by a feeling of happiness, the state of mind for which most people are inherently striving. However, when an individual is unaware of what significance truly means for him or her, regardless of how much material wealth that person amasses, he or she can wander aimlessly through life, striving blindly for meaning. Such people often will not recognize things of meaning even when they gain them, and so happiness will continue to elude them.

I have met many people who think a new car, a new outfit, or a new watch will bring happiness. As you may well know, the emotional high we experience from a material object is fleeting. It is more rewarding to seek true and enduring happiness and to have it along for your entire journey. Usually, such enduring happiness happens when there is a balance between following one's purpose and realizing one's goals and taking the time to enjoy the ride, which includes appreciating the interim accomplishments along with the many other components of a balanced life.

By way of illustration, let us say there are two routes you could take across the country by car from Boston to San Francisco. You could keep the pedal to the metal, stopping only for gas, food, bathroom breaks, and sleep, and complete the trip in several days. That would be following the "destination" mentality. Or, with your destination, San Francisco, firmly in sight, you could choose to take two or three weeks to experience the myriad places across the country that offer scenic beauty, historical significance, interesting people, adventure, fun, and much more. In both cases you would arrive at your destination, but which approach would leave you with more vivid memories and experiences, and more happiness?

Children seem to grasp this concept of the journey instinctively. Their purpose, unarticulated though it may be, is simply to grow up. Everything else is the journey itself. The thrill they take at finding a bug in the grass, the fun they have transforming a cardboard box into a pirate ship through the magic of their imagination—this is how children squeeze every bit of joy from life. They live in today. They surf the wave of the journey and find magic in each part.

It is your journey, not merely the results of your efforts, that will give you feelings of achievement and happiness. Again, one could say that happiness comes when you steadfastly pursue a goal while remaining mindful in the present to enjoy the pursuit itself.

What feels like living a life of significance to you may change over time, just as it has with our cancer survivor. As a result of her transformation, what gives her a thrill today has moved past closing million-dollar deals to helping people, often the less fortunate, to come through life-altering challenges such as the one she overcame and to remain whole and on top.

Although it required a life-threatening experience to redirect this woman's destination, she says she is now on a journey that brings forth the deepest feelings of fulfillment and happiness. Consider, therefore, focusing on the journey itself, not only the results. It is an approach that you can learn and internalize. The following exercise will help you.

For You to Consider and Do

The following simple ideas will help you to live more in the moment and appreciate the entire journey, cultivating a mindset that will bring you happiness while you also anticipate the larger goals you pursue.

1. Make it a daily habit to notice something new in your environment. Take time each day to look for something commonplace and truly observe it. It can be appealing or unappealing: a tree blossoming in the spring or a pile of garbage dumped by the side of the road—it doesn't matter. Take time to really notice it, whatever it is. Tomorrow, again notice something new.

2. While doing some mundane task such as washing the dishes or making photocopies, become aware of what you are experiencing. Focus your mind on one of your senses, such as sight, sound, or touch. Really listen to every sound of the copy machine or feel the soapy water on your hands.

3. Perform a spontaneous act of kindness every day. Whether it is a small donation to a charity at the checkout line, picking up litter someone dropped, or paying a coworker a compliment, look for an opportunity each day to make the world a more enjoyable place. If you get in the habit of looking for such opportunities, you will find yourself living more fully and more in the moment.

These three simple acts take little time and effort, but this deceptively simple mental conditioning can lead to profound changes in your ability to enjoy the journey forward.

For our millionaire hedge-fund consultant, it took the threat of losing her own life to transform her life's purpose to one that brings her immense gratification and fulfillment. Better yet, she brings fulfillment to the lives of others. Let us, then, learn from her experience and take the time to *enjoy* every step of our own journey. You are unique: until the end of time, there will never be another journey like your own. May you celebrate each step, and may happiness fill your life.

CONSIDERATION #6:
NOT SUCCEEDING VERSUS FAILING

Like success, failure is many things to many people. However, with a positive mental attitude, failure serves to be a profound learning experience...another rung on the ladder, a plateau at which to get your thoughts in order and prepare to try again.

—W. CLEMENT STONE

TIMELESS TRUTH: BOTH CURRENT SUCCESSES AND CURRENT FAILURES PROMOTE FUTURE SUCCESS.

IN THE ESTIMATION OF many, Michael Jordan is the greatest basketball player ever to play the game. In 1982 his team, the North Carolina Tar Heels, edged the Georgetown Hoyas when Jordan, then a freshman, made a game-winning seventeen-foot jump shot with seconds remaining. Later, as a professional, Jordan led the Chicago Bulls to six NBA titles, won the league's Most Valuable Player award five times, and won the league's scoring title ten times. Jordan also won Olympic gold medals twice, first in 1984 and then in 2002.

For all his success, Michael Jordan's life could have taken a very different turn. In fact, in his sophomore year he didn't make his high school varsity team. At five-foot-eleven he was deemed too short to play at the higher level. Young Jordan could have become disillusioned or bitter after not making the team. Instead, he used his failure as motivation. Years later he said, "It all started when Coach Herring cut me. What it did was instill some values in me. It was a lesson to me to dig within myself."

That "failure" was the spark that lit the competitive fire for which Jordan is well known. Between his sophomore and junior years, he became supremely focused and worked extraordinarily hard, and then he experienced a fortuitous growth spurt; the rest is athletic history.

However, for all his accomplishments, failure was something Michael Jordan continually had to overcome. By his own account, he missed more than 9,000 shots in his career, lost nearly 300 games, and missed the game-winning shot 26 times. These "failures"—or perhaps more accurately, these "not succeedings"—undoubtedly fueled Jordan's competitive nature both on and off the court. Not a great jump shooter when he entered the NBA, it was countless jump shots when no one was looking that made Jordan a deadly scorer from any spot on the court. Over and over again, the natural talent that Jordan brought to the basketball court was challenged by failure, then amplified by hard work.

We find many people like Michael Jordan who demonstrate what seems to be an effortless grace in their field. In nearly every case, however, that level of performance is the result of thousands of hours of purposeful practice of skills and intensely focused cultivation of the specific elements that go into making a superb athlete, a world-class musician, a Nobel Prize–winning scientist, an extraordinary teacher, a dynamite chef, a renowned artist—anyone who adds something of significance to our world. It is said that Tiger Woods, for example, had already invested several thousand hours of his life into the game of golf by the time he was six years old. Wayne Gretzky, arguably the greatest hockey player of all time, placed such esteem on his own work ethic that he said, "The highest compliment that you can pay me is to say that I work hard every day, that I never dog it." Successful people have an understanding that supreme effort is part and parcel of achievement, maybe even more fundamental than whatever natural talent or aptitude they may possess.

> At the height of his career, after leading the Chicago Bulls to three consecutive championships, Michael Jordan abruptly retired to devote his talents to what he hoped would be a career in baseball. He did it to indulge his lifelong love of the sport but also to try to fulfill a wish of his father, who had always envisioned his son in the major leagues.
>
> Jordan's attempt at baseball did not go as planned, and he was never more than a mediocre minor league player. But he did give it his all. He worked as hard, if not harder, than anyone else, showing up at the ballpark earlier than anyone to take extra batting practice and spending more time in the batting cage after games. Although Jordan didn't achieve greatness in the field, over the course of his year as a baseball player, Jordan's improvements are viewed as remarkable. Coaches and teammates have expressed the certainty that, had he begun a baseball career at a younger age, Jordan would have become a big leaguer.

Let us use Michael Jordan's career as an athlete to make a clear distinction between failing and *not succeeding*.

Indeed, life offers us failure as a possible outcome, and we must be thankful that it does. Consider the idea of never failing. How would we learn? How would we grow? There are so many situations in life when only trial and error can determine the answer. Without risking failure, how would we gain the experience we need to get it right next time? Also, if failure did not exist, the degree to which we experience success would not be as profound or as impactful. Indeed, the concept of failure itself allows us moments in our lives that are glorious by comparison.

Picture yourself as a runner, and at the end of every race, you are the winner. Visualize yourself as a scholar, and on every exam you receive a perfect score. Now, how about if you were a golfer, and on every hole you score a hole in one? Some would proclaim, "Awesome! Incredible! Amazing!" I once posed these scenarios to a high school assembly I addressed, and asked students to respond. One student called out, "Boring!" Of course, he was correct, and many in the room, both students and faculty alike, agreed. He knew that, besides being unrealistic, a steady diet of easy triumphs would at some point leave us feeling unfulfilled. Why? Maybe we actually love the challenge and the thrill of the hunt as much as we care for the outcome.

Failure essentially acts like your tongue: it allows you to taste victory. Failure is the element that ultimately edges success itself into the spotlight. For the reason that they both profoundly affect one's life path, we must consider just how closely related success and failure are. The following experience certainly made me realize the correlation between the two.

> For an individual to work in the financial services profession, one must pass a couple exams to gain the license to sell securities such as stocks and bonds. Like others in my field, I prepared for my license, studied all the requisite materials, and took the exam. And I failed.
>
> The experience came as a shock. It's true that 50 percent of students who take the exam experience a similar result, but I expected to pass. It appeared for a while as though my world had come to an end. I analyzed the experience over and over in my mind.

Today I view that "failure" as a pivotal point in my life, and I have come to understand that *failure* is a misused word. It is incorrectly applied to situations that are not failures at all. In reality, I did not fail that exam. In fact, I had two big successes that day: I discovered a weakness of mine, and I gained the resolve to strengthen it.

The "not passing" score I received on my first attempt highlighted my need to study more and work harder than I had expected to do. And so I dug deeper. I composed the following note to myself and posted it directly above my computer screen, where I would see it each day and receive the message that, although failures may occur, ultimate failure is not an option I choose:

> *In the moment when your vision appears to be blurred by the illusion of failure, simply realize the truth: that your vision itself remains untouched. Know that you will do nothing short of succeed and will do so on the level for which you strive. And when you do succeed, thank failure itself for testing your character. Such a moment will demonstrate how strong you are and how glorious life's moments will be.*

I read that note every day, and I reminded myself that the only way one can *truly* fail is by giving up. I could truly fail only by not cracking the books and striving to learn everything I needed to know. It worked. A month later, I took the exam again and passed with flying colors.

The next story depicts the audacity of perseverance and illustrates that perseverance is the number one enemy of failure.

At the age of seven, a boy was forced to work to support his family. His mother then died when he was nine. As a young man of twenty-two, he lost his job as a store clerk. The next year he partnered with another gentleman in a small store, but a few years after that he went deeply into debt when his partner died. He tried his hand at politics and was easily defeated in a contest for a seat in the state legislature. The next year, he had a nervous breakdown.

Two years after his breakdown, the man lost a bid to become house speaker, and by age thirty-five he had twice lost elections for a seat in Congress. After eventually serving one term, he lost his reelection bid. In his forties, things were no better. He lost a son to illness, and he lost two bids for the Senate as well as a vice-presidential nomination. However, today he is generally regarded as our greatest U.S. president.

As we all know, President Abraham Lincoln held the nation together through the Civil War and drafted the Thirteenth Amendment to the Constitution, forever forbidding slavery. Lincoln's life was replete with "not succeedings," but defeats and hardships shaped a character of such superior strength that at last he was able to alter the very face of his country's future.

So, how did Lincoln succeed? Although to the naked eye he was a person who too often lost, he was winning mentally in the grand scheme of it all. He knew to his core that when we "fail" the only salve to ease the sting and humiliation is to go on working to address the weaknesses that have been exposed. He knew that, eventually, he would master the skills necessary and transform those weaknesses into personal strengths. Furthermore, Lincoln proved over and over in the course of his lifetime that he also knew this: once we do taste success, we must still go on working, because it is always through working that we improve and develop.

Albert Einstein added that you must go on working in order to protect yourself from being corrupted by the praise that may accompany success. Whether you win or you lose, whether you succeed or fail, go on working. If you go on working, you will never fail, because failing is not when you lose, but rather when you give up after not succeeding. Your victory after any outcome will be that you persevere.

If you are worried about making mistakes, take comfort knowing that the person who never makes a mistake never experiences meaningful success. Trial and error, the learning curve—whatever you want to call it—is simply a part of the process of achievement. The number of historical examples is almost endless, and they come from every field:

Henry Ford went broke five times before he founded the Ford Motor Company.

Soichiro Honda was turned down for a job at Toyota and remained unemployed for some time before he finally started the company that bears his name, first selling scooters he made in his home.

Harland David Sanders of KFC tried, and failed, to sell his chicken recipe to an astounding 1,009 restaurants across the country before he was compelled to create his Kentucky Fried Chicken franchise instead.

Every single cartoon that Charles Schulz, the creator of *Peanuts,* submitted to his high school yearbook was rejected, and later he was rejected for a job at Walt Disney Studios.

Stephen King's first novel, *Carrie,* was rejected thirty times before a publisher finally agreed to publish it, after King's wife convinced him to submit it a thirty-first.

The Beatles were told by record company executives who didn't like their sound that guitar music was "on the way out."

Elvis Presley was told to go back to truck driving; Charlie Chaplin's act was considered too nonsensical ever to sell; Winston Churchill flunked the sixth grade; and Mrs. Edison was told that her boy, Tommy, "was too stupid to learn anything." Even Beethoven "couldn't compose"— the list of people who overcame failure and went on to change the world goes on and on.

In the wake of a "not success," one of the best things you can do is analyze what happened, how it happened, and what you could have done better to weigh the result in your favor. Rather than sinking into an emotional funk about it, use your intellect to analyze what went "wrong" and work out what you will do differently next time. If you consistently apply this approach to failures of any kind, you will soon find that it directs you toward more desirable opportunities and away from feelings of defeat.

In all cases, this truth remains: failure is an element of the success process; it places the path to success itself in the spotlight. It enlightens you about where you fall short, giving you the opportunity to transform your weaknesses into personal strengths that better equip you to move ahead. If you initially do not succeed but resolve to keep working, it is because you understand the success process. You see the "light at the end of the tunnel" and know that getting there sometimes involves what looks like an initial failure. You have identified a weakness and decided you will work on it, conquering that passing moment of defeat. Consider that the ability to appreciate and utilize failure is another attribute of the mind-set that leads to a life of value and of significance.

Make a friend of failure. Then, regardless of what you strive for, you will always: *...do nothing short of succeed and will do so on the level for* *which you strive. And when you do succeed, thank failure itself for testing your character. Such a moment will demonstrate how strong you are and how glorious life's moments will be.*

TIMELESS TRUTH: THE POWER OF FAITH IS UNRIVALED. WHATEVER YOU DESIRE WILL COME TO BE.

Optimism is the faith that leads to achievement. Nothing can be done without hope and confidence.

—HELEN KELLER

Let us first define faith as trust or confidence in oneself. There are other kinds of faith, including religious faith, but we are concerned here with belief in oneself, and the mental certainty of the *fact* that one will succeed.

I once saw an installment on the television program, *60 Minutes,* that featured a free-solo rock climber named Alex Honnold. Alex Honnold is a young man who climbs massive rock walls with no ropes or safety equipment. In other words, once he has ascended any real distance, the smallest mistake or slip means almost certain death. I sat on the edge of my couch, my jaw on the floor, watching the coverage.

Alex was ascending the iconic El Capitan, the symbol of Yosemite National Park in California. The journalist covering the story stood far enough off in the distance that she could watch his full ascent. Next to her was a climbing expert who described Alex's every move in detail. He explained that, once Alex had taken the first steps of his 2,900-foot vertical climb, there was no way to retrace his steps—literally, no turning back. Equipped only with a pouch of chalk to keep his fingers dry and what could only have been absolute faith in his ability to reach the top, Alex began his ascent. After all, reaching the top was, and always is, his only option for survival.

Cameras had been stationed along the ascent to show Alex making his climb. They provided spectacular, but dizzying, views past him and down into Yosemite's valley floor. They also provided the scenes of Alex that probably astonished me the most: he was actually whistling as he climbed, *whistling* while he was only one careless moment—one slip of his precariously perched toe, one slip of sweaty fingers—away from a gruesome death.

Here was a man who knows with absolute conviction that he will reach his goal. Because of his absolute faith in his ability, he is able to approach the task with the necessary calm it requires, thus accomplishing feats that would be impossible for virtually anyone else in the world. The slightest bit of doubt or uncertainty thousands of feet above the valley floor could be fatal. For Alex Honnold, though, the only thing between him and his goal was 2,900 feet of straight-up whistling! He literally whistles while he works.

How do we know we will succeed when we embark on a new journey? Do we know what challenges await us? What rewards we will experience? Is there any outcome that is cast in stone even before we begin?

Have you ever thought that it would be interesting to see yourself in the future, to know what you will become after some time has passed? Do you ever wish you had the assistance of a crystal ball? The idea of predicting the future has been pondered for millennia, because the future has mystified people for just as long. Although I'm pretty sure there is no magical object we can peer into and peek at ourselves in the future, I do believe there is a way for each of us to see and shape our own future. However, it is not a crystal ball but a mind-set of faith that can reveal what's in store for us.

The overarching "things" that allow you to reach success are called by various names: the Slight Edge, the Secret, the Habits of Highly Effective People, the way to the top, and many more. At the root of these "things," we see that the likelihood anyone will reach his or her goals actually hinges on and revolves around that person's faith in him- or herself (which in some cases can include his or her higher power). However you look at it, the only individual whose opinion is capable of stopping you from doing what you want to do is *you*. This is why *your* faith in *you* is what matters most.

Obviously, the future includes many variables and unknowns. Consider not fearing these things. Instead, consider embracing them with confidence. Know that strong-minded individuals who create their own futures deal with complexities, obstacles, and "not successes" daily, and they work with these things diligently to achieve outcomes of their choosing.

Unwanted variables have the potential to weaken an individual's resolve and degrade his or her mind-set. However, if you acknowledge and address unforeseen variables or limitations immediately, they can become measly factors of the equation as you continue forward. In fact, aspects of a situation that were once variables can be converted to factors that promote one's overall growth; they can even become motivators.

Variables, unknowns, the unforeseen—whatever we choose to call them, they are nothing more than small bumps placed along our paths that test our ability to maintain our confidence and fold in new information as we keep moving toward the goal.

As a very young basketball player I was limited by the lack of strength and coordination in my left hand. I really wanted to be a good basketball player, and I knew the limitations of my left hand would hold me back. Even at my early age, I had faith that I could get better if I worked at it enough, so I practiced every day, working to create a future outcome to my liking. Today, my left hand is still not as precise as my right, but it became strong enough that I was able to compete at college basketball.

Your faith in yourself and your own abilities may be one of the most powerful tools you employ in your life. It may also be the most adaptable tool in your tool chest. This intangible instrument is appropriate for you to use at any point in life and helps you prevail in every situation.

Each one of us exhibits the ability to have faith, though some of us may not realize how deeply rooted our faith truly can be. To illustrate, let's take a stroll through an average day.

Imagine each day you wake up to an alarm clock, as many of us do. Next, you take a shower, dress, eat breakfast, get into your car, drive to work, do your job, come home, eat dinner, watch some TV, surf the Web, and then do it again the next day. Well, guess what? That whole day was based on things in which you had faith, though it probably never crossed your mind.

You use an alarm clock because you have the faith it will wake you up in time to be ready for work. Is there any guarantee that it will? What if you lose power during the night? You take a shower because you believe it will make you clean and smell pleasant. What if the people you are with that day don't like the smell of your body wash? You eat breakfast, having faith that it will take away your hunger and give you the energy you need. What if your cereal is not as good for you as you thought it was? You get into your car and turn the key, having faith it will start. It doesn't occur to you that the battery might be dead. Every week you show up to work and do your job having faith that, at the end of the pay period, you will receive a paycheck. Is there any guarantee that you will? What if your company becomes insolvent in the meantime?

In your mind, there may be a guarantee that all these things will happen. Some of these things may sound silly, but bear with me. The number one reason why you believe that all these things will occur is that *you have seen similar results many times in the past.* You turn the key in the ignition and the car starts. Vrrrrroooooommmm! Off you go. You believed it would, because it has many times before. The car is functioning properly yet again.

So why don't some people bring the same outlook to their hopes, dreams, and ambitions? Why don't they see their past successes as evidence that their future goals will be successful also? Is it because their hopes and dreams are parked in the future, a time period that has not yet been seen or experienced? Is it because they don't know for certain everything that the future holds? Is it because they are trying to create something new and have not yet seen any results? Are they afraid to fail? Unsure of their ability to reach a goal? Any of these things could be true. However, the one absolutely accurate prediction we can make is, if you never try—if you never give it a shot—you will never know. Not trying makes failure the only possible option. The following exercise can help you develop faith in your own ability to accomplish what you desire.

For You to Consider and Do

1. Grab the vision of your success and hold it clearly in your mind. Write it down for best results.

2. Next, imagine your vision as a vehicle. Similar to the car that starts every morning when you put the key into the ignition, picture your vision as the vehicle that will deliver you to great success, to your hopes and dreams.

3. Now, imagine inserting a special key into the ignition. This key is your faith. And, vice versa, your faith is *key*. It is key to your future successes. It is the sustaining factor. It is more than the key to the ignition; it is the engine itself, the fuel it burns, the safety features that protect you, the steering wheel that guides you down the road of life. Your faith is both the accelerator and the brake pedal—the very things which give you control over the speed at which you advance.

The level of your faith is a driving factor in your future results. Therefore, allow the faith you have in yourself to work to your benefit; let it flourish. Your hopes and dreams are attainable—this is the truth. To succeed, you must *see with vision* and *know with faith* that this is true. If you cannot see the results now, you must have faith that they will occur—just as you have faith that your five-dollar alarm clock will wake you up.

All in all, it is easy to believe that we may not reach one or more of our goals. As children, we are taught to believe that certain goals are unachievable. Author Jeff Olson's best seller *The Slight Edge* points out that, during our childhood years, we hear the answer "No" about 40,000 times, and the answer "Yes" only 5,000 times. As a result, he suggests, our neuronal circuitry becomes wired in a way that causes us to generally believe *I can't* rather than *I can*.

It is time to consider rewiring your belief system to acknowledge that anything you can dream of is in fact achievable. It is time to consider that you *can* achieve the significance you seek, but only if you believe it is possible. The challenge before you, then, is to see the results that have not yet occurred. Faith is the tool that provides you the insight you need. Consider allowing your faith to be your "crystal ball," and look into the future, a future that you have designed.

CONSIDERATION #7:
ASK HOW AND ASK IT NOW—*CHARGE!*

The word was enough. It ran like fire along the line,
from man to man, and rose into a shout, with which they sprang
forward upon the enemy, now not 30 yards away.

—COL. JOSHUA LAWRENCE CHAMBERLAIN

TIMELESS TRUTH: SOMETHING EXTRAORDINARY
HAPPENS WHEN YOU ASK YOURSELF HOW YOU CAN
ACHIEVE A GOAL RATHER THAN TELLING YOURSELF
YOU CAN'T.

AS AN INCOMING FRESHMAN AT Bowdoin College, I decided it would be a good idea to attend a guided tour of the college to gain some insight into its rich academic history. As I strolled through campus and marveled at the buildings, a story my tour guide told became one I would always remember.

Joshua Lawrence Chamberlain was a professor at Bowdoin College in the years before the Civil War. A brilliant linguist who was fluent in nine languages, Chamberlain had at one time or another taught every course in Bowdoin's curriculum other than those in science and mathematics. When war broke out, he felt a calling toward joining the army to defend the Union.

Although both his grandfathers had served in the Revolutionary War, Chamberlain himself had no military training. However, he made no secret of his political views and felt strongly that the Union cause was just and the country must remain united. Not everyone on the faculty shared his view, and under the false pretense of taking a two-year leave of absence to study languages in Europe, Chamberlain promptly joined the army.

As you may know, he gained lasting fame at the Battle of Gettysburg on July 2, 1863, based on a single courageous decision he made in what would become a decisive battle of the war.

Colonel Chamberlain and his 385 men were positioned on top of a hill known as Little Round Top at the extreme left flank of the Union forces. His orders were not to let any Confederate soldier pass his side.

The first Confederate attack on Little Round Top occurred in the early afternoon. Chamberlain and his 20th Maine Infantry regiment were able to force the opponents to recede. Not long afterward, however, a second, third, and then a fourth attack commenced. With each attack that afternoon, the Confederate soldiers were able to draw closer and closer to the line that the 20th Maine was ordered to hold. By the time the fifth attack began, Chamberlain's force was fighting with a fraction of its original manpower.

There was no hope of reinforcements, because the rest of the Union army was likewise heavily engaged. As the rebel forces mounted for yet a sixth attack, Chamberlain's men were nearly out of ammunition after the long afternoon of battle. Colonel Chamberlain knew their situation was precarious and that no reinforcements were coming. Yet, Chamberlain still needed to fulfill his duty: to protect that line.

The Confederate army was under the command of General Robert E. Lee, who had proven himself nearly invincible. Lee's army had inflicted defeat after defeat on the Union army as he took the fight from Virginia into Union territory in Pennsylvania. Morale in the North was flagging after so many defeats. Had the Union lost at Gettysburg, General Lee could easily have turned his army eastward to Washington, D.C., and the outcome of the war might have been different.

Retreating from Little Round Top in failure simply wasn't an option. As history shows, this action could have decided the pivotal battle in the rebels' favor. Although the 20th Maine was now at an extreme disadvantage, Colonel Chamberlain nonetheless asked himself *how they would win.*

History does not tell us whether Chamberlain knew the significance of the orders he was about to give. Certainly he was aware that, if the Confederate army breached his flank, the entire Union army could have been encircled.

Faced with his options, none of them good, Chamberlain realized that his only hope for success lay in one audacious strike. He ordered his men to affix their bayonets and then... *CHARGE!* All of a sudden, down the hill stampeded the 20th Maine, straight at the rebel force. The offensive strike confused the Confederates, who mistook the boldly charging soldiers as fresh Union reinforcements. Chamberlain's actions and the deception they created had astounding results. In the ensuing melee, the Union army was able to not only successfully defend its position but also capture hundreds of Confederate soldiers in the bargain.

The third day of the Battle of Gettysburg saw the tide turn to the Union's favor, and Lee and his forces eventually retreated back into Virginia. The Confederacy never recovered from the defeat, and a marker in the Gettysburg National Memorial commemorates the "high water" mark of the South during the war, the farthest point that Confederate soldiers were able to penetrate into Northern territory. For his leadership and courage at a pivotal moment, Joshua Chamberlain became a war hero and many years later received the Congressional Medal of Honor.

Chamberlain was appointed to oversee the Confederate parade of surrender as the rebels laid down their arms and colors in April 1865 at the Appomattox Courthouse, and he later wrote a stirring recollection about the events of that day. His inspiring words are worth reading, and I have included Chamberlain's account of the ceremony in this book's appendix (see page 193) as a reflection of this great leader's depth of character.

Today, Joshua Chamberlain is remembered by millions, and his statue stands at the entrance to my alma mater, the college he left to follow his calling. Although he is best known for his courage in battle, in his postwar roles as governor of Maine, college president, and entrepreneur, Chamberlain undoubtedly asked himself many times the same question he asked on that hot July day at Gettysburg: "How will I accomplish what must be done?"

Consider making it your policy to ask yourself how you will achieve an objective rather than asking yourself whether you can. Avoid telling yourself you cannot; don't rationalize your success away by saying the task is too difficult or even impossible. Sometimes it may appear as though you have nowhere to run and no possible way to win. In these cases especially, you too are obligated to do something. Don't let yourself off the hook: ask yourself what it is that must be done.

To succeed, to win at life, you must act, and sometimes you must act fast. You always have options. Sometimes the options are unfavorable. Work with what you are given, and make the best of it. Having faith in your ability to handle whatever comes will make it easier to see the best direction to go. As always, the *inner you* holds the answers; like Joshua Chamberlain, you simply need to ask how, then *charge!*

TIMELESS TRUTH: PROCRASTINATION CAUSES ONE TO STAND STILL. WHILE YOU STAND STILL, THE WORLD IS MOVING FORWARD, AND THEREFORE YOU ARE ACTUALLY FALLING BEHIND.

What is not started today is never finished tomorrow.
—JOHANN WOLFGANG VON GOETHE

Procrastination runs counter to a proactive approach, which is counter to building a life of significance. The Civil War lends us another historical case in point.

> General George B. McClellan was a leader of the Union army during the early years of the war. He possessed excellent organizational skills and was considered a military genius by many. However, a weakness for delaying decisive action hampered him throughout his career and may have prolonged the Civil War by years.
>
> In 1862, for example, General McClellan saw a golden opportunity to capture Richmond, Virginia, the capitol of the Confederacy. He delayed taking action, however, and then the window closed when the Confederate army was able to implement more defenses for the city. Had McClellan acted quickly, his force, along with another Union army, could have executed a pincer maneuver against Richmond, an attack it could not have withstood.
>
> Later that year, at the Battle of Antietam, the Union army outnumbered General Robert E. Lee's Confederate army two to one, and Lee's unfortunate forces had their backs to the Potomac River. During the battle, however, General McClellan was slow to respond to Lee's much quicker movements. General Lee's outnumbered army quit the battle

and withdrew across the river to Virginia, but even then McClellan delayed and didn't pursue him aggressively. Lee was able to regroup and expand his army, and the war would drag on for another two and a half years.

General Robert E. Lee was a worthy opponent, and to waver at a critical moment against him was a serious miscalculation. President Lincoln eventually replaced McClellan with another general who he felt would act with more decisiveness. Lincoln, frustrated at McClellan's continual delays, once remarked that he didn't want to take McClellan's army away from him, he just wanted to borrow it for a while. After all, the Confederate Army had almost won the war under General McClellan's leadership despite being outnumbered by more than two to one.

It's not that General McClellan didn't have justifications for his hesitancy, but its net result was procrastination. Because his many missed opportunities prolonged the Civil War, military historians do not rate him highly as a battlefield general.

Not everyone's procrastination has such large-scale and disastrous effects, but procrastination is something that affects all of us at times. Have you ever heard somebody discuss a goal he or she has, explaining in passionate detail this worthwhile thing he or she wants to achieve, but then this person never does anything about it? We've explored many reasons why this happens; procrastination is another one.

Some people tend to be forever preparing for the "test" or the "journey" or the "big leap." However, the first step is one they never take. Why? Fear of rejection? Fear of not succeeding? Are they scared of what the future holds? Are they perfectionists who delay because no result will fit their ideal?

Whatever there is to be afraid of, consider that not taking the first step is the greatest risk of all. Procrastination, putting off that first step, amounts to *not taking it at all,* and as we've already discussed, the fact of not trying is the true failure. Not trying allows unfulfilled potential to be constantly in your life.

Procrastination is the mismanagement of potential. Think of it as short-circuiting your own plan for success. Conversely, consider the magic in simply starting. Once we begin an endeavor, incredible things can come into play; forces unimagined can impact our progress and, ultimately, support our success.

General Joshua Chamberlain obviously would have failed at Gettysburg had he not taken bold action at a perilous moment. With virtually nothing to work with, he pulled a victory out of thin air. General McClellan, by contrast, had the very capitol of the Confederacy in his crosshairs but let his finger falter on the trigger. Lacking the proactive outlook of Chamberlain, McClellan was unable to take advantage of an opportunity to end the war and spare three more years of carnage.

You and I may never find ourselves in such historically pivotal moments. Still, it behooves us to learn from the example of Chamberlain, the great war hero, and be warned by the legacy of McClellan, a capable but ultimately mediocre figure. Let McClellan's challenges inspire in us the tendency to get started, to take action and get the ball rolling.

There is a saying in the life insurance business: "Procrastination is the highest cost of insurance." Premiums will be higher later than they are today. Similarly, for all of us—the college student anticipating the labor of a term paper, the army general fearing a bad decision, or those of us trying to make progress on our goals—the price we pay later is often much higher. Decisiveness is one of the most admirable of all personal attributes: no matter what you are attempting, when you get on with it, it tends to work out better than when you have delayed.

Studies demonstrate that the majority of people fall on the McClellan side of the fence most of the time. One study estimated that up to 75 percent of college students considered themselves procrastinators.

Essentially, procrastination means putting off a task that is important by doing things of lower priority or of greater immediate interest.

Imagine you are a student with a paper to write that accounts for half of your semester grade (and perhaps you are). Imagine that instead of getting down to work, however, you check your emails, talk on the phone with a friend, do your laundry, and update your Facebook status, all activities that are in some way necessary and justifiable, but that are clearly of a lower priority than getting to work on the paper and doing a first-rate job. Sound familiar?

The reasons for procrastination vary from one individual to another. Low self-confidence may prevent individuals from beginning a task they are not sure they can adequately do. Some people rationalize procrastination by claiming they are too busy with other tasks. Quite possibly they are—one is always doing *something*; the procrastinator simply isn't doing what he or she knows should be done first. Some people enjoy the stress of working under a tight deadline. Others knowingly delay tasks to prove to others that they can't be bossed around. Whatever the reason for it, procrastination always exacts a common penalty: it steals our precious time—and wasted time is something we can never get back.

Certainly, the effects of procrastination on one's life and relationships are anything but desirable. The tolls of chronic procrastination include lost opportunities, needless stress, frenzied activity to meet deadlines, substandard products, resentment from others, strained relationships, and even self-loathing for having allowed oneself to be controlled by this negative tendency.

The good news is, there are effective ways to deal with procrastination. One of the most significant and workable methods is explored in Consideration 2, where we discuss the importance of identifying our inherent purpose in life. People with a passion for what they do are less likely to procrastinate. In the wise words of Confucius, "Choose a job you love, and you will never have to work a day in your life."

If you never feel as though your work is work and you truly love what you do, each task before you looks less like an obstacle. A person's drive to "get it done" is usually higher when the task itself is something he or she finds satisfying. If procrastination is a significant issue for you, consider once more the For You to Consider and Do exercise starting on page 44. Working a job you don't like, much less love, or enrolling in a major that does not align with your life's goals creates an environment that is almost certain to promote procrastination.

For You to Consider and Do

There are specific actions you can take to overcome your tendency to delay what you know must be done.

1. Clarify in your mind exactly what needs to be accomplished. What should be done first? Specifically, what is the activity of the highest value for you to embrace right now?

2. After you identify the top-priority task, think about it in more detail. Imagine you have to write a quarterly report for your business: Thinking "I need to write a quarterly report" is far too general. Exactly what aspects of the business need to be covered? Whom is the report for, and what do they expect to learn from it?

Once your end product is clearly defined, you will be able to streamline the steps toward finishing it: in the case of the report, you can omit unnecessary research, data gathering, writing, and so on. Clarifying the matter at hand goes for any task. For example, say you need to clean out the garage. Before you begin, give some thought to exactly the result for which you are going. Is it having all the kludge removed and brought to the dump and recycling center, or do you simply need to organize? Do you want the floors painted? The windows washed? Removing the feeling of generality associated with a task will make it easier for you to strip it down to action steps and tackle any job head on.

3. Once you have your goal firmly in mind, list the steps necessary to accomplish it. Although your goal must be firm, your sequence of steps for reaching it should remain somewhat flexible. If you aren't flexible about the order and definition of your steps, any roadblock or external delay becomes a perfect opportunity to put the task on hold—in other words, a license to procrastinate.

For example, let's go back to your quarterly business report: Imagine you need to collect some information from a colleague to include in the report. You go to his office and find that he will be out of town until next week. Instead of heading back to your desk to play Angry Birds, consider a more flexible plan. Who else can give you the needed information? Can you email or call your colleague or someone else and get it that way? Are there aspects of the report that aren't dependent on that information, that is, steps that you can work on now?

With your goal clearly defined, you will find a way to reach it if you remain flexible yet determined. You have probably done this when driving: you are trying to get to work, but a road crew is making improvements to your normal route, so you take different streets and still make it to work on time. Flexibility applies to advancing all goals, big and small.

4. Insofar as it is feasible, do the entire task in one chunk of time. It makes much more sense to paint an entire room in

one go rather than the walls today, the ceiling next month, and the window trim the month after that. If you were to add up all the time cleaning brushes and rollers, shifting furniture around, and setting up your materials to continue on the project, it would become clear that it's far more efficient to do the entire job at once. The same is true of other tasks. The objective here is to eliminate duplicative functions, which only use up valuable time.

5. If the task is lengthy, you may become exhausted physically or mentally if you stay at it too long. When you need a break, take a break. Benjamin Franklin once advised that a day should consist of one-third work, one-third rest, and one-third recreation. To recharge your batteries for productive and efficient work, you may need those other two-thirds of the day. Remember, life is about balance, and we work to live, not live only to work.

Moving forward on any task of importance requires you to make lots of decisions. What needs to be done? How long will it take? What is the goal? What resources are needed? How should you go about it? All these questions require that decisions be made. A state of indecision can bring things to a rapid halt. Those who cannot make up their mind about which way to go will stand still. And so will their project or company, or even their life.

Just as there are solutions for procrastination, there are solutions for indecision. One method is to simply gather more information about what needs to be decided on. When you have learned enough about all aspects of the situation, the right decision to make becomes clear. Once it is clear, as we learned from Colonel Chamberlain and General McClellan, the trick is to *act on it*.

Imagine you cannot decide whether to take a new job with another company. There must be factors on either side of the balance that seem to be of equal weight; otherwise, you would have either handed in your resignation at your current job or else declined the new offer. Consider gathering more information about the new position as well as your future prospects at your current company. More information may unlock your ability to decide.

Sometimes not initially succeeding at a task can discourage us and cause us to put off a follow-up attempt. But do you remember Thomas Edison's vast number of "unsuccessful" attempts before he managed to create his inventions that we still use to this day? (Revisit Edison's story in Consideration 3.) Each disappointing result could have served as an excuse for the inventor to procrastinate on his next effort or even to give up. However, from each new attempt, Edison learned of something that didn't work. Thankfully, Edison knew how to view "failings" as part of the inventing *process,* and he expected such results—perhaps he even *welcomed* them. Certainly, Edison knew how to use not succeeding as a motivation to try again.

All in all, consider making a conscious effort to eliminate procrastination from your approach. If you banish it from your list of tendencies, you will develop the ability to make higher quality, proactive decisions. A strong ability to decide and the ability to do so without procrastinating will speed you on your way.

Rather than ask *if* you can achieve a goal, ask *how,* and then don't delay: charge ahead!

CONSIDERATION #8:
THE IMPORTANCE OF GENEROSITY AND TAKING AN ACTIVE INTEREST IN OTHER PEOPLE

To laugh often and much; to win the respect of intelligent people and the affection of children...to leave the world a better place...to know even one life has breathed easier because you have lived. This is to have succeeded.
—RALPH WALDO EMERSON

TIMELESS TRUTH: YOUR GENEROSITY WILL BRING FULFILLMENT TO YOU AND OTHERS.

ONE OF THE MORE MEMORABLE parables I've picked up is *The Go-Giver,* a short, sweet, and impactful book co-written by Robert Burg and Dr. John Mann. This story teaches how easy it is to become a better giver and highlights why giving is so important. *The Go-Giver* and its "Five Laws" have the potential to positively impact your mind-set and your approach to your goals. This is why I am offering the Five Laws for your consideration, along with some thoughts about why and how each can be so powerful and why you might consider incorporating these principles into your own daily life.

1. The Law of Value—*Your true worth is determined by how much more you give in value than you take in payment.*

To understand its raw power, this law requires an honest assessment of yourself. It asks you to take a moment to clear your mind and peer inward, thoroughly searching within yourself to identify what specific value you have to offer—whether at work, at home, or in a social setting. Everyone has it within themselves to contribute to the greater picture of society. With this in mind, ask yourself, "What is the greatest value I have to offer?"

When reflecting on this question, know that the definition of "value" is fairly broad. By itself, the term *value* holds different meanings for different people. Therefore, consider approaching this law from a thousand-foot view.

For instance, being of value could mean spending time with a child, serving as a positive influence. Perhaps contributing value is taking a portion of your paycheck to buy groceries for a deserving stranger at the community food bank. Your value could be expressed in sharing your happiness with someone who is feeling sad. One aspect of your value could be in sharing ideas and creativity that empower a friend or a stranger. Ultimately, you are having a positive influence on the lives of others.

Regardless of how you choose to define value, consider that you have something of merit and importance to share with the world. Everyone does. Consistently challenging yourself to identify what value you can offer to the lives of those around you is the secret to effectively implementing the power of this law. Albert Einstein had a firm grasp on the idea of value. He stated, "You should strive to become a man of value rather than a man of success." His reasoning includes not worrying about what you will get back: if one strives to become a person of value, success will inevitably follow.

Einstein's philosophy relates nicely to that of noted author and speaker John C. Maxwell, who consistently and eloquently touches on the importance of value in his description of how to be an optimum leader. Maxwell has said, "People want to be around you because of your reputation and what you represent." This is an attribute that Maxwell determined is found in a "Level 5" leader. Not to be confused with the

Five Laws of Giving, Maxwell's levels of leadership are classified from Level 1, someone whom people follow because they are required to do so, on up through intermediate degrees to the pinnacle at Level 5, an individual whom people follow because of the leader's character and what he or she represents.

These quotes from Einstein and Maxwell resonate, not only because they came from distinguished and unique minds, but because each acknowledges the universal truth that an individual's value is like an individual's currency. People will "price tag" your worth once you show them (through your actions and your influence) your individual value. People typically prefer to be surrounded by those they know, like, and trust—and by people they can count on. These characteristics are the inherent traits of a true leader, and they are also the characteristics of an individual who brings genuine value to the lives of others.

We have all heard the expression a million times: "You reap what you sow." Consider that if you always sow and maintain relationships with people based on truth, integrity, and value, you will forever be associated with such characteristics. Simultaneously, you will be providing value to others. Your value and the truth and integrity you express are derived from your individual flow of generosity. *Generosity is the root of value!* Being generous with your time, money, ideas, and happiness augments your value to others, and this will bring you far. Your generosity to others will open doors to amazing life experiences and thrilling opportunities. The more often you give, the more often you will witness the growth of those around you and experience the positivity this brings. What a feeling!

Consider the simple fact that most people enjoy being around those who make them laugh and feel good, wanted, and accepted. Human beings are wired to desire the feeling of acceptance. We have a desire to be wanted and needed. These feelings are rooted deep in the foundation of our human existence. Maya Angelou, the noted American author and poet, captured this aspect of human nature when she said, "People will forget what you said and will forget what you did, but they will never forget how you made them feel."

What better way is there to impact how someone feels than by giving them something of value, such as yourself and your talents, your leadership, your uplifting perspective, your optimism, your kind words, or your shoulder to lean on in a time of need? The rewards of sharing your time, your ideas, your happiness, and your sincerity with others will far surpass the "value" of any monetary payment you will ever receive, and far outstrip any dubious advantage you might gain by withholding these gifts.

Have you identified the greatest value you have to offer? So often we minimize the value of doing the little things. Value need not come in large packages. Often the smallest gestures yield the most rewarding value.

Take a minute to consider the following question: If someone makes you laugh until your stomach aches and tears run from your eyes, how much is that worth? Really stop and think about it. Now try to place a monetary value on that feeling, that emotional sensation that creates such a rejuvenating moment for you. You might say it's impossible. Good— it is important to know that the reason things such as your memories and your happiness are priceless is that there is actually no relationship between them and money. These types of wealth are invaluable, and they are also yours for eternity; you can never be robbed of them, at least not by somebody else. Things of real value, things of true worth, by definition will be priceless and enduring.

Consider, then, building your wealth of things other than just money, including precious experiences and memories. Memories will always be with you, and exchanging value with others through shared experiences builds true wealth, in their lives and your own.

When I think about what contributes true value to life, I often visualize an old man in his final years, sitting on a bench and pondering his life and all the memories he has amassed. I visualize all he has accomplished in his life and what aspects of his accomplishments would remain and still satisfy him at this point. I assume that, at his advanced age, he would probably not be racing sports cars nor care whether he ever wore an expensive suit. I imagine he may not care right now whether he did or didn't own a mansion at some point or if he wears a Rolex that keeps the same time as any other brand of watch. At this moment in his life, even if he could afford to, he may not be about to scuba dive in Caribbean waters, and his body may not allow him to do many of the things he enjoyed throughout the years.

The obvious question becomes, then, what *is* this man able to do and enjoy? What will he take with him when he leaves his active role in this world, after the physical capabilities of his young body slip away? After he no longer has his work? From my time and conversations with my mentors, I have come to believe the answer is this: He will use his time to reflect on all that he did, all that he accomplished, all that he shared, and on the relationships he built. The impressions that he made on people and the changes he made in the world will forever be a part of him. In other words, this is the time in life when he will examine the butterfly effect of his life's efforts.

The butterfly effect, of course, is the theory that seemingly insignificant changes early in the life cycle of an event can result in major effects in the late stages. The fluttering of a butterfly's wings in Brazil could, the theory goes, result in a hurricane in the Gulf of Mexico. In other words, my old man on a bench will reflect on how his actions affected the progressive movement of things and people in this world, hopefully toward the better.

To cultivate the blessings of life that hold true value requires diligence, sincerity toward others, and constant effort. When I say "blessings of true value," I'm referring to things that cannot be taken from you, such as positive experiences. Therefore, give plenty of them to other people and to yourself. Give happy memories to everyone you know; besides giving you enjoyment, it will assist you in becoming a person of value. In turn, your ability to provide continuous value will inspire people to like and trust you. Grounded in integrity, your generosity will make you an automatic and continual success.

2. The Law of Compensation—*Your income is determined by how many people you serve and how well you serve them.*

From this law you will learn that, if you want more success, you must find a way to serve more people. Truly, there is no secret to becoming wealthy in any part of life, be it the area of finances, relationships, friendships, family, creativity, or anything else. Provide those around you with generosity and an abundance of positive energy, and you will find that your individual, emotional, spiritual, and financial spheres will flourish.

It might not be an expected avenue to personal success, especially financial success, but nonetheless consider this: providing genuine service with no thought of receiving something in return is a sure road to a better life for you (yes, even financially) and for everyone with whom you deal. Motivational speaker and author Zig Ziglar may have said it best: "You can get anything you want in life if you help enough other people get what they want."

Again, remember the simple fact that people enjoy being treated politely and with respect, and therefore, this kind of treatment is something for which they are looking. The legendary boxing trainer Angelo Dundee was fond of saying, "It doesn't cost anything extra to be nice." Most everyone likes to be acknowledged as a person who has something of value to offer. In addition to giving people the recognition they want, it is also one of the kindest acts you can perform to help them identify the value that lives within them (including their own kindness) and then inspire them to share it with the world.

If you know that someone has something to contribute, to share with the world, tell that person! Promote him or her, and acknowledge and praise that person for his or her strengths. In other words, consider letting yourself "manage up": empower yourself to promote the growth of those around you, not only your peers or subordinates, but your superiors as well. There are many simple ways of serving others.

Granted, a go-giver mind-set runs counter to the self-centered habits we have learned, first as children before our worldview expanded to include others, then as we grew older and became bombarded with the "me first" values our society holds. It may require a conscious shift in your approach toward others to begin serving them in the way prescribed by this law. You may have to remind yourself to compliment someone on a job well done before it becomes a habit to do so, but practice paves the way for awesome results, and like any skill, you become better at serving others the more you work at it.

The ways you can serve others are limited only by your imagination and willingness. Opportunities, big and small, are all around you. At work, for instance, when a coworker is carrying a box to storage, you hold the door open for him. A new employee appears lost: you show her the ropes around the office and invite her to lunch to make her feel a part of the team. Someone is having a problem with a project, so you truly listen, seeking to understand all factors involved so you can give helpful advice. Truly serving your coworkers, your boss, your vendors, clients, or customers, and family and friends makes you indispensable and all but guarantees you not only great personal satisfaction but also material promotions of many kinds, including greater income.

The benefits of service accrue in less obvious ways as well. Outside of work, you can donate clothing, appliances, or equipment you no longer need to charity. You can give a recently finished book to someone who may need to hear its message. Consider giving up your seat on the bus or subway to someone who looks as though he or she had a long day. Something as simple as picking up a piece of trash feeds the habit of serving others. None of these actions costs you a penny, but the invaluable positive energy generated from such acts soon becomes a natural part of your personal environment. People will take notice, and as like attracts like, good things will come your way.

It is true that a rising tide lifts all boats, including your own. By serving others, you become the rising tide that lifts everyone in your environment.

3. The Law of Influence—*Your influence is determined by how abundantly you place other people's interests first.*

President John F. Kennedy once urged Americans, "Ask not what your country can do for you—ask what you can do for your country." I believe what President Kennedy acknowledged is a timeless truth: your life offers you more when you offer more to the people in it.

As Maya Angelou has told us, the people you meet during your life will remember you according to how you made them feel. They will always associate you with a certain feeling and with a level of comfort. Make that feeling happiness, and make people feel at ease. If you bring people something of value, the positive feelings you instill will not be forgotten. The best way to generate such feelings in others is through leading a selfless life.

Someone once told me (and probably you too) that our success hinges on not *what* we know but *who* we know. Take that statement a step further: our genuine influence is determined, not just by who we *know,* but by how much *interest* we take in them. If you treat people as though they are truly special to you, they will always remember that. Even further, it is important to remember that it's really who knows *you* and *likes* you that holds weight. What ultimately matters is how the people around you feel as a result of your presence, your time, your words, and your actions. Therefore, always consider putting other people first.

4. The Law of Authenticity—*The most valuable gift you have to offer is yourself.*

Now consider this: the most valuable gift we are given is our time—and it is finite. It is an unavoidable truth that at some point everyone walking around today will be gone. The only question that should matter to any of us, therefore, is how we invest our time.

We will live this life only once, but we each have the potential to make it a great and rewarding life, one that creates a legacy that lives on long after our time has passed. Did we enrich the lives of others? Did we create a legacy, or will we be forgotten? Whose life will be better tomorrow because of what we did with ours?

Tomorrow, when you step out of bed, remember that you are mortal. The day will come when the final chapter of your life will be written and your "book," the story of your life, will be finished. As you consider this, ask yourself a simple question, "Would people want to read my book?" No matter how large or small the impact you leave seems, its effects will go on indefinitely. (For more about your perpetual impact, give *The Butterfly Effect* by Andy Andrews a read.)

Together, you, your time, and your efforts can write a magnificent epic that leaves a message for others and from which they can learn. Just as all the particulars in life are subordinate to the fact of life itself, all things you accomplish and say are subordinate to the person you are. "No stream will rise higher than its source" is a piece of wisdom worth remembering.

Part of exhibiting your own authenticity is to take an interest in others. As John C. Maxwell has said, "People don't care how much you know...until they know how much you care."

Someone whose very career is a lesson in authenticity is Mike Krzyzewski, coach of the Duke men's basketball team. The hard work, dedication, and passion "Coach K" brings to his job has led him to the peak of his profession as the winningest coach in the history of men's collegiate basketball. Yet success on the court has never been paramount to Coach K. As he says, "Making shots counts, but not as much as the people who make them." These words capture his coaching philosophy in a nutshell.

Because relationships are the most important thing to him, Coach K values the truth above all else. He puts it like this:

> In our program, the truth is the basis of all that we do. There is nothing more important than the truth because there's nothing more powerful than the truth. Consequently, on our team, we always tell one another the truth. We must be honest with one another. There is no other way.

Make no mistake, though: all is not warm and fuzzy inside the Duke program. When Coach K recruits a freshman, he says, one of the hardest things he has to do is to break the player's old habits in order to turn him into a team asset. To do this, Coach K and the player may go through trying times. By conducting grueling practices and putting himself in the players' faces 24-7, Coach K brings these young men to the point where, even though they may hate his guts in certain moments, he wins their trust. They trust him because he does what he says he is going to do, every time, no matter what. Once Coach K has the trust of the players, each becomes a believer in his way of doing things, but more important, they become friends for life.

The individual star players Coach K recruits to Duke become a squad of warriors who will fight for the benefit of the team. He accomplishes this by showing how much he cares and how much he is a person of his word. Once his players truly see this, they then begin to care more about his considerable basketball knowledge.

All in all, Coach K puts his best self forward for these young men, and he knows that his best self is his authentic self. The result of his authenticity and the time and energy he invests is an environment that nurtures camaraderie among these young men and creates a future of winning, both on and off the court.

In life, you are the source. You are the one who dictates everything *downstream*. You, meaning the best you, the authentic you, are the person responsible for building all you have envisioned and all that reflects the deepest layers of your inner self. Consider that your inner self gives rise to your ability to cause someone else's cup to overflow. Someone once gave a demonstration of this truth that left a lasting impression on all of us who saw it.

My business partner and I were at a dinner with a man we had recently hired as an agent for our company. After the meal, the conversation turned to the topic of perspective.

Our new agent explained one of his life philosophies: we each hold a certain perspective and viewpoint regarding just about everything that surrounds us. However, our perspectives are sometimes, as he said, "inside the box." To demonstrate, he held up a glass that was a bit more than half full of water and asked us what we saw.

A number of us wisely answered that we saw a glass that was half full. It turned out his point, however, was not to reinforce the well worn cliché about having a positive outlook. Instead, our business associate explained that people often look at exactly what is given, or what is literally right in front of them. He said that the amount of water in the glass was only enough to fill a glass halfway because of the perspectives we held on the potential of a certain amount of water relative to a specific glass.

Our associate then reached across the table and grabbed an empty glass that was half the size of the first, and placed it in the middle of an empty dinner plate. While holding the half-full glass of water high above the smaller glass, he said,

"This water has more potential than you considered simply because you were comparing this amount of water to this specific glass. However, when I pour this water into the smaller glass, it proves that this amount of water is more than capable of filling someone else's cup."

As he spoke, he poured the water from one glass to the other, causing the smaller glass to overflow, and the abundance of water flooded the plate and then the dinner table. It was a beautiful mess he made and his point was profound.

Each of us has something abundant nestled in our deepest layers that can cause another's cup to overflow.

A key to helping others along their journey is being authentic. Consider giving your all, no matter what you are doing and no matter whom you are doing it for, whether yourself or someone else. At the end of the day, the authentic you is the most powerful, influential, and inspiring you. Consider sharing that person with the world.

5. The Law of Receptivity—*The key to effective giving is to stay open to receiving.*

I have witnessed time and again that, when one is receptive to advice, mentorship, help, and suggestions, one's own ability to be helpful increases markedly.

"In my walks, every man I meet is superior in some way in that I learn from him," said Ralph Waldo Emerson. By accepting this timeless truth on our journey through life, we remain open to receiving all the knowledge and wisdom we need, both to achieve our wildest dreams and to support others in their own journeys.

While we are growing up, we are given all manner of useful advice, knowledge, and wisdom from parents, teachers, coaches, counselors, clergy, family elders, upperclassmen, friends, superiors at work—the list goes on. The practice of mentorship has been around at least since the ancient Greeks and undoubtedly much longer. There is no question that cave men demonstrated the art of shaping stone axes to younger members of the tribe. Without the apprentice system during the Middle Ages, none of the great cathedrals of Europe would ever have been built. Mentorship is one of the primary means by which civilization has progressed.

Emerson's sage statement advises us to be receptive to others and to allow the people in our lives who have so much to give, and who are willing to give it, to cause our cups to overflow. The weekend I spent talking with Philip aboard his boat certainly did that for me. (To revisit other lessons from Philip, see Consideration 1.)

Opening yourself to the knowledge and perspectives mentors have to give is one of the best ways to flatten your learning curve and accelerate your growth. At times, one may feel as though asking for advice or help would deal a blow to one's pride. In these cases, remember the Chinese proverb, "The man who asks is a fool for five minutes—the man who doesn't ask remains a fool forever."

Consider identifying your mentors, then ask for their advice and be prepared for your cup to overflow. Most will be only too glad to help, and in the end, the secret to your success may be as simple as a mentor's answer to the question, "How did you do it?"

You need not reinvent the wheel or rediscover fire. Simply find someone who has reached your desired level of achievement and then make their methods your own. Duplicate what they did, in your own individual way. Add your own sense of self to the templates for success already available to you, and the results will be everything you envisioned and more.

All the knowledge in the world is available to us if only we remain open to it. The more knowledge we expose ourselves to, the more wisdom we amass. The wiser we become, and the better at what we do, the more capable we are of sharing ourselves and our strengths with others. Mentors and their wisdom serve as the sparks to a self-perpetuating mechanism of positive influence that enhances the quality of our journey and the quantity of our significant moments. Consider that being open to advice is what will eventually allow you to constructively give your own.

To understand and measure the true power of these five laws, you must consistently implement them. Together, they will help you to see how generosity is part of the larger process that enables you to realize your potential.

TIMELESS TRUTH: TO REACH YOUR MAXIMUM POTENTIAL, PEOPLE MUST KNOW YOU, LIKE YOU, AND TRUST YOU.

To realize your fullest potential, consider letting others see what lies *within* you and not just what is on the surface. For others to see the inner you requires more than simply hearing your name or meeting you in person, more than gaining minor insight to what you do professionally or recreationally.

Think of the three people with whom you are emotionally the closest. Now ask yourself why you are close with them. What type of connections do you share with these people? What made your connections with them as strong as they are today? How did you come to truly understand what motivates them, what brings them joy, what causes them sadness, and what propels them to impassioned growth?

Is it the result of many common experiences? Is it the result of long conversations during which you created a bond that became unbreakable? Was it being there to lean on when support was needed? Is it because you know you can trust each other? On one level, it is probably all these reasons and others. At its core, though, the bond you share is that each of you feels that you truly know who the other is inside, and each knows the other cares about the real him or her.

Because you earned your confidantes' trust, they opened up to you and shared a part of their inner depths. The result is one of the greatest gifts life has to offer: strong relationships with other people, which happen to be an element found at the core of almost every success story ever written.

I was once told that life is all about relationships, and I believe that it's true. I'd add that success is all about relationships, too. No matter what you want to accomplish, other people will be crucial to the process. Relationships are what open the doors to effective collaboration, mastermind alliances, shorter learning curves, accelerated growth curves, not to mention the unrivaled feeling of human connection, and other astonishing results.

As you have experienced, a relationship typically begins with something as simple as a conversation. Two people are introduced somehow. They begin to converse. A connection is either found or it's not, and the rest takes a natural course. Or does it? Is it possible to find a way to connect with just about every person you meet? Although I can't tell you the answer, I do know that there are ways to increase the likelihood of making a connection. Often you can forge a connection by doing nothing more than taking an active interest in another person's life during a simple conversation.

To arrive at that "aha moment" when you know you are on the path toward a life of significance, however you may define that, consider applying the "know-like-trust rule." It takes a level of understanding about another person to earn his or her sincere respect and to position yourself to positively influence his or her life. If you do eventually earn a person's respect, it is likely this person will want to learn more about you as well. In time, the people you have taken an interest in may come to view you as someone they know, like, and most important, trust. As a result, they may even acknowledge you as a friend. What an honor!

I developed a mnemonic device you can use to explore your connection and commonalities with other people. It is called "C.H.A.T."

143

C.H.A.T. can help you create a bond with any person you meet, and it can be used all the time. It supports the practical application of one of Dale Carnegie's most important teachings from his famous book *How to Win Friends and Influence People*:

> Why talk about what we want? That is childish...and absolutely absurd. Of course you are interested in what you want. You are eternally interested in it. But no one else is. The rest of us are just like you: we are interested in what we want. So, the only way on earth to influence other people is to talk about what they want and show them how to get it.

C.H.A.T.—A Simple Conversation that Leads to Extraordinary Results

Carnegie's words illustrate the importance of focusing on the wants and desires of other people. C.H.A.T. is a device that will help you do exactly that: discuss what is important to the person in front of you. It will enable you to look within the people you meet to see who they are and to understand what is important to them, what drives them, and even what holds them back.

C is for *career*. You can learn a great deal about other people and their individuality by doing nothing more than asking them about and then listening to them speak about their profession. You will discover as you listen that people will tell you the ups and downs associated with their job. They may explain how they got started, when the major transitions took place, and why each occurred. You may hear people readily discussing their passions and what things of value their career has brought to their lives. On the flip side, people have usually also realized from experience what they do not enjoy, professionally speaking, and this is equally important for you to understand. You will gain insight about what drives each person and what holds each back. You will begin to understand what is important to him or her and what is not.

H is for *home*. Mothers, fathers, brothers, sisters, grandparents, aunts, uncles, cousins, friends, and of course, location all add up to this next category. Friends could be defined as "the family you choose." Home is a place where the bonds between parents, children, friends, and relatives as well as cherished memories are formed. Home is the *place* where the heart grows fonder. A person's current home may not be in the same location where he or she first grew roots, but often a childhood home is a place that still exists in the heart and will always seem near, no matter the distance in miles.

Gain an understanding of where people grew up. What state are they from? What city? What was it like in that city during their childhood? Did they live in a neighborhood full of kids with whom to play? Did they have a childhood nickname, and what's the story behind it? What about their school? What was it like? Who was their best friend growing up? Who was their favorite teacher and why? What did their family do for fun? How often do they get back home to see old friends and family, if they have since moved away?

There are numerous questions you can ask someone about his or her home and family and friends, any of which can generate a conversation that lasts for hours. You will also soon realize that a discussion about family inevitably segues you easily into the other topics of C.H.A.T.

A is for *activities*. What does the person do for fun? Does she like the outdoors? Is he more of the indoor type? What activities does he or she enjoy the most? Do they include hiking, skiing, swimming, attending sporting events, fishing, traveling, following a favorite band, exploring different cultures, staying at home and surfing the Web, playing billiards, doing puzzles? It is your job to find out. Determine what someone truly enjoys doing and then, most important, come to understand why. Once you know, find a way to connect on this topic by discussing the commonalities you share.

What people choose to do in their free time is often indicative of what they are most passionate about and what is most important to them. However, individuals can have very personal and thus varying perspectives on the virtues of the same activity. Consider, then, making it a priority to fully understand not only what they do for fun but also what it is they love about their activities of choice. This one topic alone can tell you a great deal about a person.

Lastly, **T** is for *time*. This aspect of C.H.A.T. is a technique, not a topic. It simply reminds you to take the time to listen, thus making your conversations natural and leisurely. Display a sincere interest in what others are saying. Let the person with whom you are speaking know he or she has your attention. When the other person is speaking, make strong eye contact. When the person makes a statement, acknowledge it, and then follow up with a question that encourages him or her to share more.

C.H.A.T. can be used anywhere, anytime, and with anyone. It can be used with family members and complete strangers, and it allows you to demonstrate to any person you speak with that you are interested in him or her—that you would like to know more about his or her life, thoughts, worries, passions, goals, and ambitions. It allows you to build rapport and to demonstrate your level of trustworthiness.

I was once advised to always trust selfish interest, to always rely on the fact that people will go after what is important to them. And there lies a timeless truth. Once you know what people are after, you are better able to understand their actions and their motivations. It is only then you can truly assist each in his or her endeavors. That is, you must know specifically what people want if you plan to help them get it. And when you have been able to help a person accomplish his or her goals, you will have become an influence in that person's life not soon to be forgotten.

Once people know you care about them and their interests, you can begin to experience some of the greatest gifts life has to offer, such as friendship, companionship, trust, and even love, as well as the great satisfaction of collaboration and striving for mutual benefit. You can begin to form relationships that last a lifetime with whomever you engage. If you approach life in this way, you will soon have relationships and friendships in abundance.

A life of significance is all about relationships. Tomorrow, when you meet someone new or are sitting with an old friend, consider giving generously of your time and attention. Have a C.H.A.T., then see what unfolds.

CONSIDERATION #9:
YOUR TIME IS A COIN

Time... you can't own it, but you can use it. You can't keep it, but you can spend it. Once you've lost it, you can never get it back.

—HARVEY MACKAY

TIMELESS TRUTH: THE TIME WE HAVE IS FINITE AND INVALUABLE.

WHILE AT BOWDOIN COLLEGE, I took many science courses and learned fascinating things about the physical world, including the transformations our planet has undergone and the expected changes to come.

During one of my sophomore biology classes our professor compared the timeline of the planet Earth to that of mankind's existence on it, in order to bring time itself into perspective. She asked us to guess: "If the entire history of the Earth were represented by one 24-hour period, how long would human beings have been around?"

Students' heads twisted from side to side, looking around to see if someone in the class had the answer. A few students took a stab at it, but apparently no one was coming close. At last, our professor answered her own question: "The last few seconds of the twenty-fourth hour." The silence in the lecture hall was complete.

For me, the professor's comment made me realize something completely off topic: a person's time is the most valuable asset he or she has. I thought, older people tend to have much more tangible wealth than younger people, but younger people have what older, wiser people tend to consider a far more valuable asset: time.

After class that day, a friend and I began a discussion about work, particularly the pay a person receives in exchange for his or her time on the job. I mentioned that, once you receive your paycheck for that week's work, you will never see another payment for those forty hours again. My friend agreed and said that this is how it works for everyone. I shared with her the lesson from that day's biology class regarding the age of planet Earth. I added that the average life expectancy of a human being is seventy-seven years. Seventy-seven years— that is roughly all the time we have to experience the infinite beauty of this world and to create a legacy, to imprint our mark on it.

My friend and I discussed the value of income and ways in which we might be able to determine our own monetary worth in a rewarding career. We discussed simple economics: supply and demand. We agreed that our time on Earth is finite, and yet the number of years each of us will actually live is unknown. We tossed around ideas about how little time we truly have, thinking of every analogy we could to place this short supply into perspective. As we dug deeper, what seemed to be a heightened sense of awareness began to creep in for the two of us. We concluded that our time is exactly like a coin: it has value, and it is ours to invest however we choose. Further, we concluded, our time's value is incalculable; therefore, our choices about how to spend it are of the utmost importance.

Simple economics would dictate that an item of such great importance but such small quantity would have a demand that is outrageous and, therefore, a hefty price tag. Both literally and metaphorically speaking, time is in such short supply and high demand, its value should be through the roof. And I believe that this is the case.

We continued our conversation in the context of my friend's summer job. Theoretically, we said, each day when she gets up and goes to work for someone else, she is allowing them to determine how much her time is worth in the form of her pay. I did not learn what my friend earned per hour, but according to the theory of supply and demand, it was way too little—as my friend already agreed.

Ask yourself this: how can you put a price tag on someone's time when everyone on Earth has a finite and unknown amount of it? Isn't it infinitely valuable? You are the only one who knows what your time is worth to you, and therefore, you are the only one who can put an accurate price tag on it. Your time is exactly like a coin. As we all know, a single coin is not much; we must therefore treat it with respect and spend it mindfully.

Therefore, consider investing your time wisely by sharing it with those you love, by doing the things you enjoy most, and by forging memories that you will enjoy for your entire life. Look for the best value in the career you choose, in the friends you keep, in your recreational activities, and in the time you spend helping others reach their goals. Leverage the value of your time and squeeze every bit of experience from it that you can. This coin—your small window of time—is all you have. Think of it as the most extraordinary and most valuable coin ever minted, the most valuable asset you will ever possess.

Because we never know how much time we actually have, it may help you grasp the preciousness of your time by thinking of how you spend it in a single day. Imagine that, each day when you wake up, you find a shiny new gold coin next to your bed. It is yours to spend however you wish, but it only lasts a day; you can't save any part of it for tomorrow and neither can you borrow tomorrow's coin to spend today. It will be spent no matter what, but will it be wasted? You do have choices. Although you can't put off spending your coin, you can invest your coin wisely today in things that do last, and allow it to pay you all kinds of dividends tomorrow and in the following days. Conversely, you can just as easily fritter it away.

The coin that appears beside you each day when you rise is the twenty-four hours you have been granted, and although your time on the planet is like a single grain of sand on a never-ending beach, consider that without it the beach would not look the same. In fact, consider that without your contribution the beach would be extremely different.

The greatest investment you can make is to offer the world the first-rate version of yourself. Everybody has a purpose in life, and we all create an impact with our time and actions whether we choose to or not. Your mere existence generates effects. By doing what you are good at, and what you are great at, you contribute so much more to the larger picture. Therefore, create your own legacy and impress your mark on the world. Do so by investing your time shrewdly.

To transfer the concept "your time is a coin" into the day-to-day reality of jobs and paychecks, it is important to understand that your professional worth is sometimes not instantly reflected in the form of a paycheck and dollars. Rather, it is reflected in the person you are becoming, the wisdom you are gaining, and the experiences from which you learn and grow and then invest in your future. Rather than merely counting your dollars per hour or week, then, think also of your "lifetime dollars," and consider whether they are being well invested.

TIMELESS TRUTH: YOUR PROFESSIONAL VALUE WILL DEPEND ON HOW YOU INVEST YOUR EXPERIENCES INTO YOUR OWN FUTURE.

In ages past, people bartered. They exchanged eggs for wheat and arrowheads for pelts. This, of course, had potential drawbacks, such as when one did not want arrowheads but the other sorely needed pelts. As you well know, over time a substitute for goods came into use: currency, or money.

The first broadly known forms of money were commodities, such as barley in Mesopotamia and shells in Native American societies. Later, gold or silver coins became more universal, making trade easier. Goldsmiths in the Middle Ages issued receipts to townsfolk who deposited their gold with them for safekeeping, and these receipts also functioned as currency. Over time, the exchange value of these receipts became standardized.

Today, the hours you work at your job are exchanged for money in the form of a paycheck or an electronic funds transfer that is wired directly to your bank account. From there you can use the money in the form of cash or check or another electronic transfer to pay your bills and spend as you choose. Most people I have spoken with, the great majority in fact, would like more of this thing called money. It seems many of us are certain that more money will make our lives easier and better and make us feel accomplished. My friend Ben is one of these people.

Ben is now twenty-five years old and works as a mechanic for a local garage. Every week, Ben brings home a paycheck in exchange for the fifty hours he worked. Every so often I hear him complain about how he is not being paid enough to do his job. However, what Ben does not realize is that his paycheck does not accurately reflect the value he received from the hours he put in. His paycheck actually reflects much less, because his entire pay does not come in the form of today's dollars. Actually, Ben brings in a lot more each week than he thinks he does. He simply hasn't seen the other things he earns or turned them into more money yet.

After hearing Ben voice the same thoughts three weeks in a row, I felt compelled to discuss the value of his paycheck with him in light of a piece of advice I had received myself a few years prior. I began by mentioning that the number of dollars paid to him on his check is his own choice. When I said this, he looked back at me in shock, as though he had maybe seen a ghost.

"How do you figure that?" he asked, with an eyebrow raised. He went on to explain that he works fifty hours per week, and that for his efforts his boss cuts him a check based on an hourly rate that his boss set.

I explained that the amount of his pay was a choice because of his own decision to work for someone else. When you work for someone else, you allow them to tell you the rate at which you will be paid. "There is an abundance of value in this, however," I added, hoping to shift his perspective.

I shared with him what I had been told a few years earlier: The truth is, in the larger picture, much of our "pay" is not coming to us in the form of a check with a dollar amount on it. Rather, it is coming in the form of education. For Ben, and for many of us, it is coming from the experiences we have each day and the new tricks of the trade that we are learning.

I told Ben that maybe he needed to view his employer as a mentor, not just a boss. I shared that mentors are people who shorten learning curves and accelerate growth curves. We discussed that, if he were to take advantage of his mentor's leadership and make the most of the apprenticeship-type environment he is in, Ben would soon find himself positioned to have his own shop, able to hire his own staff and determine his own compensation.

Ben is gaining the experience today that he will use down the road to build his own business, with his own mechanics and his own systems. The knowledge that he amasses and the success of his own future business will demonstrate his true professional worth, and *that* is the additional compensation he had lamented not receiving.

It is natural to look at people who are successful and choose aspects of their lifestyle that would be enjoyable to have. For Ben, he found this easy to do with his boss. However, what is not as easy as lamenting your position is to take inventory of your own assets and privileges and to create and implement the game plan for attaining your needs, wants, and desires. This requires time, much thought, consistent effort, multiple areas of expertise, and many other factors discussed earlier.

Achieving the paycheck you desire may require an ingredient mentioned in Consideration 3: vision. Again, vision is the ability to see your future results as if they have already occurred instead of only dreaming about aspects of a different future. Vision is the ability to know what it will take to achieve a certain goal even without ever having attempted it before. Vision is what allows you to see the end result even when there is nothing tangible in front of you to prove it will become a reality.

Every day when we wake up, we face challenges, opportunities, obstacles, and choices. The bottom line is that decisions must be made. As Jeff Olson explains in his book *The Slight Edge*, you either move forward in life or you allow yourself to slide back. The world is constantly changing and moving forward. If you are not growing with the world as it progresses, then you are falling behind, even if ever so slightly. The same is true about life experiences. If we are not investing our current life experiences into our future, always building on what we have, we are missing the boat. Consider utilizing all the tools and experience at your disposal to grow as much as possible in the short time you have.

In today's competitive society, we must prove ourselves; we must prove our worth and our value to others. We cannot expect other people to give us the things we want. We must work for what we want, and it is while working that our skills are developed and honed. Therefore, pay attention to whether you are growing or falling behind. Pay attention to the experiences you have on a day-to-day basis, and ask yourself if they are creating a "better you." Ask yourself whether what you accomplish and learn each day is making you a more valuable asset to your company, your family, your friends, and yourself. When you focus on making the answer to this question affirmative, the paycheck in your hand will always be larger than it appears.

If you plan to stay at your job, consider envisioning your paycheck as the paycheck you are choosing for now. Consider that your worth and value will show in time and that there is no substitute for experience. Consider that your week-to-week paycheck represents only a portion of your professional worth and of the monetary value you generated. It is up to you to pull the residual value from within yourself.

Now you can consider our next timeless truth:

TIMELESS TRUTH: MONEY *CAN* BUY TIME.

Once you have the paycheck you desire, a new question arises: Can money buy happiness? The jury tends to say no, not directly anyway. We will discuss the prospects of *indirectly* buying happiness in a moment.

Psychologists and social scientists have explained that, although it is true that richer people tend to be happier than poorer people, this is only true up to the point that their and their family's basic needs are supported. Additional income that funds a lifestyle above and beyond the necessities has only a small effect on levels of happiness.

People making high incomes tend to aspire to make more money, but as we just heard, once they have achieved basic stability, they may have reached the limit of what money can do for their sense of well-being. Additionally, people often pursue more money at the expense of enjoying the very things or experiences that once brought them happiness. In those instances, acquiring more money can actually *reduce* their level of happiness.

Some research demonstrates that simply showing a picture of money to participants in an experiment significantly lowers their appreciation of simple pleasures. Studies of lottery winners show that hitting the jackpot does not increase the lucky winners' happiness levels and, in fact, renders them less able to enjoy simple pleasures such as a cup of coffee with a friend.

Money, then, may not be able to buy happiness. However, there is one thing I know it can do: it can buy you time.

To explore this truth, let's pretend you and I just took a quick financial inventory of your household cash flow. Let's say we determined your income over the course of a month and determined your expenses over that same period. We calculated the difference between your earned income and your expenses to figure your disposable income.

Say, for example, your income is $3,000 per month and your expenses are an equal $3,000 per month. Given these circumstances, you have few options regarding work tomorrow: you must show up or face financial hardship in the near future. At this point, you do not have a disposable income.

Now, imagine you work overtime the following month and make $4,000. You have now earned yourself $1,000 of disposable income, assuming expenses remain at $3,000. Imagine doing this every month for years. Imagine that the $1,000 of disposable income you earn each month is placed into a bank account or, better yet, invested. Imagine that over the years your account's value grows slowly yet steadily.

By working hard and working smart, by sacrificing certain things now, you are giving yourself the wherewithal to buy time in the future. What do I mean when I say "buy time"? Essentially, by investing the fruits of the hours spent working today, you are stockpiling hours you can spend tomorrow going about life exactly as you please. If you have enough money saved from years of hard work, at some point you may not have to work at all to meet your financial commitments. The money you have in the bank and invested will allow you to stay home or travel or enjoy other aspects of the lifestyle of the financially independent.

The magic trick here is obviously spending less than you make. This requires discipline and forethought and is one of the very best habits you can develop in your financial life. Today, readily available credit, such as that offered by credit cards, gives people the ability to spend more in a month than they will make, but they are buying only short-term gratification at the expense of a financially sound long-term plan. You could say they are actually stealing time from their future selves, who will have to pay off the debt they've incurred. If you can find it within you to delay gratification until you have the means necessary to buy the next thing you want, you will develop one of life's most valuable habits.

If you create the financial means to buy time, you will be able to spend that time doing whatever your heart desires. If you can do whatever your heart desires, this is likely to include the things that bring you the most joy. Perhaps in this way money can buy happiness.

May your paycheck be the paycheck you choose, your activities be the ones you desire, and may you invest your valuable time in a way that pays you dividends in the future.

CONSIDERATION #10:
CIRCLES OF INFLUENCE

When we honestly ask ourselves which person in our lives means the most to us, we often find that it is those who, instead of giving advice, solutions, or cures, have chosen rather to share our pain and touch our wounds with a warm and tender hand.

—HENRI NOUWEN

TIMELESS TRUTH: THE PEOPLE WITH WHOM YOU ASSOCIATE AFFECT THE PERSON YOU BECOME.

THERE WAS A YOUNG GIRL named Stacey Thomas who grew up in Michigan and whose passion was sports, particularly basketball. Her love for the game was so great that her brother, older by three years, often let her tag along when he met his friends for a game on the playgrounds of Flint. Stacey often managed to get herself into the game and found herself challenged to keep up with the older boys. This soon became her sporting environment, and she was forced to adapt to it or risk losing the outlet for her passion.

Stacey's burning desire led her to work hard and improve her basketball skills to the point where she not only kept up with her older competitors but thrived. She thrived so well, in fact, that she became a star at her high school, then a record breaker in college. She went on to a successful career as a professional in the WNBA. She even won a WNBA Championship.

The foundation of Stacey's athletic success was laid as a youngster as she learned to keep up with her circle of influence. Stacey's elder brother and his friends could be considered the young girl's first sporting mentors. They may have been reluctant at first to let her play, but they didn't shut her out of their circle. They undoubtedly taught her much about how to play the game, and as she improved and demonstrated that she belonged, they accepted her fully and took great pride in her ongoing success and development.

Whether they knew it or not, this circle of mentors gave the girl everything she needed: a little help, a little hope, and a splash of belief.

As adults, too, we all have circles of influence, those networks of social relationships that influence us through example, guidance, advice, and pressure as well as in many other ways, both positive and negative. The most important thing we can do is become aware of our circle and design it to be one that increases our likelihood of success in whatever endeavor.

As we begin to form our circle of friendships and acquaintances, it becomes only a matter of time before we are influenced by the people in it. It is a natural tendency to pick up on one another's habits, manners of speech and word choices, recreational activities, and more. We begin to share more and more in common with those with whom we spend the majority of our time, and as a result, we often become emotionally closer to them. It is when we begin to share our deepest feelings and concerns that we begin to receive their advice, sometimes whether we ask for it or not.

It is important to acknowledge that everything we experience affects us in some way, and we can be especially vulnerable to the opinions and advice of others. That said, how do we know when someone else's advice truly is the *best* advice? The answer is, we don't. However, we do not *need* anyone's advice to be "the best advice." Advice is something that should be used only to spark original thought and to bring our own feelings and knowledge to the surface. It is within us where the answers exist, so in itself, advice is neither good nor bad. It is how we translate the advice and what we do with it that determines its value.

People often lend advice based on their own life experiences, and make no mistake, these can be invaluable to hear. For certain, it is one of life's luxuries to rub shoulders with people from professions unlike our own, who have had different life experiences and who hold viewpoints contrary to our own. It is from such individuals especially that we can learn and grow in ways, and at speeds, we never imagined. The noted American novelist Nathaniel Hawthorne went so far as to say, "It contributes greatly towards a man's moral and intellectual health, to be brought into habits of companionship with individuals unlike himself, who care little for his pursuits, and whose sphere and abilities he must go out of himself to appreciate."

However, the truth is, despite the various and valuable perspectives you gain from the experiences of others, you are the only one who knows what "feels right" and what "just seems to make sense" to you. You are the only one who truly knows what makes you happy, what you are passionate about, and what makes you feel fulfilled. You know what choices will move you forward and which will hold you back. These are the factors, not the advice or opinions of others, that should drive your pursuits.

In his masterpiece, *How to Win Friends and Influence People,* Dale Carnegie asks his readers:

> Don't you have more faith in ideas that you discover for yourself than in ideas that are handed to you on a silver platter? If so, isn't it bad judgment to try to ram your opinions down the throats of other people? Isn't it wiser to make suggestions and let the other person think out the conclusion?

The late Jim Rohn, noted speaker and author, was once asked by an audience member in a Q&A session, "I like the approach of [author X] and wonder if you recommend that I adopt his ideas?" Rohn replied, "Rather than give you a yes or no on that, I suggest you read multiple books on the topic. Then you decide." Do consider the advice from Dale Carnegie and Jim Rohn when making conclusions, and derive your own!

The well-meaning college counselor who advises you to become a lawyer may not know you well and be unaware that your passion and aptitude is in working on automobile engines. If you took his advice, you could soon find yourself three years into pre-law classes, studying law books, governmental policy, and legal contracts, and living a life far from what you envisioned or consider your "dream life." Again, you must follow your own instincts about what advice is right for you, but nevertheless *quality* advice can be just what you need.

You can gain great perspective on your situation from sound advice from the right source. How, then, do you position yourself for sound advice? Let's come back to circles of influence. Simply put, we must be aware of who we surround ourselves with, being sure to fill our lives with people who share common interests and those who understand us for who we are.

Analyze your social affiliations, and you will begin to realize there are some people with whom you are more compatible than others. Spending more time with these people will strengthen your relationships with them almost effortlessly. Each will become a closer friend and grow to know you better. Each will become more familiar with how you function and with your strengths and your challenges. As a result, these people will be well positioned to make fundamentally sound suggestions that are more appropriate for you.

It is difficult to find people who have your back, who are there through thick and thin. It can be a challenge to differentiate those who are loyal and sincere from those who are not, but over time you will gain a clearer understanding of the role each person in your circle should play moving forward.

Many people begin to adopt habits and interests similar to those of their closest friends. If you begin to spend more time with people who golf, you too will probably pick up the game. If you begin a new job and your new associates often get together for wine tasting on Friday nights, it is likely that you will begin to go wine tasting more often than before. Unfortunately, if the people in your work environment also tend to use foul language quite freely, you are likely to pick up their ways of speaking too.

We are by nature easily affected by the people who surround us, so isn't it therefore imperative to surround ourselves at all stages of life with people who will lift us up and give us solid guidance when needed? Consider flooding your social circles with people who will pick you up when you are down, efficiently redirect you when you veer off course, and who will hoist you even higher when you triumph. These are the people you want to include in your circles of influence.

For You to Consider and Do

The question naturally follows: how do we find such people?

1. Try sitting down with pen and paper and actually listing some traits of the type of person you want in your social circle. Do you want ambitious go-getters? Easygoing, gregarious types? Sincere empathetic personalities? You may be the driven type who could benefit from the balance that an easygoing friend could bring to your life. Conversely, you may see a need for a few competitive types in your circle to spur you on.

Often, our friendships grow out of the context we find ourselves in. We meet people at school or around the neighborhood or at work, then over time and through repeated interactions we become familiar, and a friendship evolves. What I am suggesting instead is to take a more proactive approach to including people in your circle of influence, people who may provide you with more of what you want and need.

2. Once you have thought about what you'd like your circle of influence to look like, make plans to find the people who will create it. If you want to meet go-getters in your profession, look for a convention or workshop that would attract that type of person. If you are looking to meet people for social fun, look for events that match your interests. Just as I suggested that you actively hunt for the answers to your deepest questions in life (see Consideration 1), consider molding your circles of influence in a way that will benefit you in your search for significance. And don't think of this as selfish: remember, you are striving for a life of meaning, and those you associate with will rise with you.

On our journey, we come into contact with many types of people. Perhaps just as important as selecting those we wish to accompany us is understanding which types of people we are better off without. For certain, there are toxic personalities and people who can drag us down. It is sometimes best to simply distance ourselves from these types of people; otherwise, we run the risk of being influenced by their counterproductive attitudes and behaviors.

Consider being a person who attracts relationships to your life that are mutually beneficial. Part of this is appreciating such people when you find them; nurture your relationship with them and cherish it.

Simultaneously, consider being at least as enthusiastic a giver as a taker in these relationships. It will only serve to strengthen your circle and all those involved.

To create the most appropriate and positive circle of influence possible, decide what is important to you, then search for people who have common sets of goals and a similar moral fiber. Possibly include people who can bring balance to your circle with a perspective or attitude you may lack.

Similar to our champion woman basketball player, if you want to improve at basketball, play with others who are more advanced than you. You will ensure success in your pursuits especially by surrounding yourself with those who are more advanced than you in the areas where you want to excel. Simply, if you want to make more money, work with people who make more than you do. Examine what your superiors are doing, and to a certain extent, mimic their professional habits, consider their advice, understand their belief systems, and then prepare for similar results to unfold.

It will behoove you to identify your true friends and positive circles of influence. For in the end, your circles of influence play an important role in the development of the person you are becoming. Consider filling your life with people who can serve as mentors, and just as the man behind the velvet rope promised, "your cup will overflow."

CONSIDERATION #11:
ONE BALL AT A TIME

To get through the hardest journey we need take only one step at a time,
but we must keep on stepping.

—CHINESE PROVERB

TIMELESS TRUTH: ALL GREAT THINGS TAKE TIME.

LIVING A LIFE OF TRUE significance does not happen overnight. Obviously, a life of value and meaning cannot be purchased in a store, and it does not come in a bottle. It must be strived for constantly, and yet no effort is more worthwhile.

A few years ago, I took a trip to Denver, Colorado. At twenty-five, it was the first time I had seen that part of the country. Simply put, Denver is a beautiful, sparkling city with the majestic Rocky Mountains as a backdrop, and seeing it was unforgettable. Equally as memorable is what I learned while there.

I understand that I am, to some degree, a clone of the people with whom I associate the most. I therefore place myself around people who are positive influences and who can shorten my learning curve toward higher achievement. I have always valued learning from people who are "seasoned veterans," those who have been through the "school of hard knocks." Why? Their experience speaks volumes.

In July of 2009 I landed at Denver International. There to pick me up was my friend Roger, a sixty-two-year-old business associate and insurance mentor. As I walked through the airport doors toward the street, I saw my ride: a classic 1978 Rolls Royce with a chauffeur standing at attention.

"Welcome to the Mile High City," Roger said cheerfully.

As Roger and I began to pull away from the airport, he began to discuss the plans he had made for the week. It was then that I first noticed one of Roger's dominant personality traits: he pays strict attention to detail and applies a methodical approach to everything. To put it another way, he pays close attention to *why* and *how* he does anything.

Roger grew up on a farm in Illinois, where his family raised cattle and hogs. At the age of twenty-three, he realized he wanted something different out of life. So he packed his things and headed for Colorado.

Over time, Roger has built a strong business practice that is worth millions, and he has the type of reputation in the insurance industry that is both respected and sought after by people in the field who are hungry for success. Today, he has a family with two beautiful daughters, and he has his health. For many reasons, he can live his life however he chooses, but the most significant reason is that he has worked extremely hard for a long time to make himself financially free.

Roger is passionate about what he does and performs every task keeping in mind that great success is not easily achieved. Roger knew at a young age that building and maintaining a life of significance requires a certain mind-set and consistent effort. I soon learned that Roger applies his philosophy relentlessly, regardless of the endeavor.

After a thirty-minute drive from the airport, we arrived at Roger's home. I quickly changed, and we were off for dinner at Elway's, a restaurant owned by Denver sports legend, John Elway. On our way home, we quickly discussed plans for the following day. Actually, Roger did not tell me what we would be doing. However, he told me to be up and ready at 6 a.m.

"Six in the morning?" I asked. "For what?"

Roger just laughed and said, "You'll see!"

Morning came before I knew it, and Roger was pounding at my door.

"Let's go, let's go, let's go," he shouted from the foot of my bed.

He was showered and ready to go, and I still had one eye shut. I asked again what the plan was. He looked at me, laughed, and said, "Jac, we have balls to find!"

"Balls to find?" I yawned.

Roger explained that right past his backyard was a golf course, and every day he loved to walk the course for his morning exercise. At this point, I still didn't understand what this had to do with finding balls, but he soon made it clear.

He took me out to his garage, opened the door, and— wow! I couldn't believe my eyes. There were boxes upon boxes, baskets and baskets, jug after jug, and container after container, full of golf balls.

"I picked up every single one of them," he said with a smile and a tone of pride.

I was stunned. I wondered how long would it take one person to find that many golf balls. It must have taken years. Holding the image from his garage in my mind, I headed for the course with Roger. It became clear we were on a mission, and he soon made it into a multiday competition. That day,

Roger found the first ball, and he was sure to let me know.

"There's one," he called out enthusiastically from a hundred yards away, his newly found treasure held high in the air. I thought to myself, *This guy has lost his mind*. Every ball he found caused him to do the same thing: he raised it high in the air, counted it aloud, and handled it as though it were pure gold. In his eyes, it was; they all were. And his madness didn't stop there.

After that first day out, we made our way back to Roger's garage. We counted the balls we had found. Eighty-six. Not bad for a morning walk. The second morning came, and we were back at it. This time, something else happened, something so unexpected that I questioned what I saw.

Roger and I had been walking along a cart path chatting about a number of different things when I suddenly noticed I was talking to myself. Roger had been right beside me, talking and laughing, and then all of a sudden—poof! He had vanished. I spun in a circle, but Roger was nowhere to be seen.

I began backtracking, and as I came around a set of thorn bushes, there he was, digging through trash cans on the golf course.

"Roger, what are you doing in there?" I yelled.

With his arms still in the trash, he looked up at me with a face red from struggling to reach the bottom of the bin and said, "We need containers to put all these balls in."

Again, I was confused. As he began to walk toward me, I could see golf-ball sleeves in both of his hands. Roger explained, "People are crazy. They throw money away all the time." *People are crazy alright,* I thought. I asked Roger about his plan regarding all these balls; there were so many in his garage that he could never use them all.

"I am going to sell them," he said with great enthusiasm.

But why did he treat every ball he found as if it were the most special thing he had ever put his hands on? I just had to ask; I had to know.

"Roger, every ball you find and every container you dig out of the trash excites you so much. Each one is only a ball, and each container is just a worthless paper and plastic sleeve." He stared at me for a moment, and then he said something I will always remember.

"Jac, I have over 50,000 balls in my garage, and they were all found one at a time. If I didn't find this ball that I hold here in my hand, I would only have 49,999 balls. And that is the principle behind why I do it. It is my work ethic. All great things take time. Rome was not built in a day. Every ball is special, and every ball is a part of the bigger picture."

At that moment, there stood in front of me a man who is worth millions, who would not have to work another day in his life if that is what he chose, and yet he was digging through trash cans for containers to hold golf balls that are worth a dollar each. However, a dollar each did eventually become $50,000. Clearly, for Roger it is not only that the last ball put him over the $50,000 threshold, or that the 30,000th ball brought him to $30,000. Rather it is that Roger's mindset and consistent work ethic, practiced at all times and applied to everything he endeavors, has inevitably resulted in the freedom and opportunity to live his life exactly as he chooses. In his case, this includes hunting for golf balls.

Forrest Gump said that life is like a box of chocolates. I say that life is like acquiring 50,000 golf balls: it happens one ball at a time. Therefore, be methodical and consistent in your approach toward your goal. Acknowledge the big picture, and know that the end result will occur as long as you continue to envision it and strive for it, then dig into the small steps that will take you there. Consider that you may have to do the same things over and over to build the larger picture, but know too that each effort is its own unique contribution.

Without the first ball, the journey has not begun. Pick up every ball you find along your journey and know that it is adding to your stockpile. Without each and every ball from the first to the last, the end result can't be as great. Consider approaching life in this manner, attacking your small tasks and large goals with this level of tenacity, and I promise you this: you will attain whatever it is that you desire. Ball by ball, you will build a life of significance.

CONSIDERATION #12:
A NEW TWIST ON AN OLD CLICHÉ

The clichés of a culture sometimes tell the deepest truths.
—FAITH POPCORN

TIMELESS TRUTH: YOU SHOULD LIVE EACH DAY AS IF IT WERE YOUR LAST.

AT THE AGE OF SEVEN, I started to clutter the walls of my bedroom with pictures and posters of my favorite athletes. Michael Jordan, Nolan Ryan, Mickey Mantle, Larry Bird, Dr. J, and many others all had their spot on my walls.

As I grew older, the number of posters increased. When I finally set foot on campus at Bowdoin College, I began a new collection that consisted of prominent philosophers, scientists, and musicians as well as legendary athletes. One of the posters I had was of James Dean, with a quote at the bottom that read, "Dream as if you will live forever, live as if you will die today." That poster now hangs in my garage next to many others that I have admired over the years.

I have endeavored to live in consideration of the advice on that James Dean poster. In my mind it is saying, "Think big and go after your dreams—starting right now." Or, at least that was the message I thought it conveyed, until in the spring of 2011 when I met a rousing lady named Laura who instantaneously tilted my angle of perception.

Born in October 1936, Laura was diagnosed with type 1 diabetes at the age of fourteen. She was told by medical experts that she had approximately fifteen years left— only fifteen years to capture her dreams and carry out her life's purpose. Notwithstanding the disheartening reports that would continue to clutter her medical history, Laura somehow found the ability to charge her life with both passion and grace.

She fell in love with a young man, and they dragged clinking tin cans behind their car and started a family together, never knowing when that last grain of sand would slip through the neck of Laura's hourglass. Her and her family's motto became "Make the most of every day." Most of the plans that Laura and her husband made over the years revolved around the belief that Laura would soon predecease her husband. However, as Laura told me and as time has proven, science and medicine only go so far—and then there are miracles.

Today, at seventy-six years young, Laura is a volunteer subject under observation at the Joslin Diabetes Center in Boston. She is a member of an exclusive group of people from around the world who undergo specific tests aimed at determining why they have been able to survive type 1 diabetes for so many years.

During one of my enjoyable visits with Laura, she looked at me after listing all the medical complications she has experienced over the years and then, without batting an eye, told me that she has been blessed. *Blessed? Living your whole life on a medical roller coaster? How is that a blessing?* I couldn't help but wonder at her ability to feel this way.

Throughout her entire life, Laura has never known when her clock might stop ticking. She said she realized that, in reality, none of us really knows when our time will be up. This thought led Laura to her life philosophy, which she shared with me:

"Rather than living each day as though it is your last, live each day as though it is everyone else's last."

Her remark sent chills over my entire body; I grasped her meaning immediately. Laura explained that, when you live life by this model, you genuinely place the interests and well-being of other people first. She believes that giving is one of the secrets to finding meaning in life; staying open to receiving is another. Because of the approach to life Laura developed, because of her optimistic beliefs, attitude, personality, and joviality, she has attracted many wonderful people and blessings to accompany her through the years.

After a story like this, I had to ask Laura her secret to solidifying a positive attitude amid such discouraging odds. Laura replied, "My secret is 'the nine Fs': family, friends, faith, fun, feistiness, philosophy, physicians, fruit, and fiber." She then added that in the past, every time she revealed her secret to someone, her late husband would always chime in, "You know, Laura, you never could spell."

Laura's words of wisdom were straightforward, and she delivered them in a sincere and serious tone, and yet she had a playful look in her eye when she shared her husband's comment. I am convinced that the twinkle in her eye symbolizes the importance of always looking for the good in any situation.

In the face of her medical complications, Laura adopted a different approach to life, a twist on the message from my James Dean poster. Laura's approach is not only go-getter but also altruistic. Laura's story is unique and special, not only because she has outlasted her life expectancy by forty-nine years, but also, and most important, because of how she has entertained those forty-nine years. The positivity that she has been able to generate, harness, and share while facing such disappointing odds is truly remarkable.

I have hung a new poster in the garage. It is self-made, with simply the following words on white poster board: "Dream as if you will live forever, live as if each person you know or meet may pass today." It owns a spot right next to Mr. James Dean.

Laura, you are right: you have been blessed from the very beginning! We all are. May Laura *continue* to drink from the saucer, and may you too live life to the fullest, every single day.

THE WAY FORWARD

Many people chase after success. Others pursue money.
But I think the happiest people on earth are the ones who
have found significance. The real question of life must be,
what has significance for you?

—ANONYMOUS

TIMELESS TRUTH: IT IS ALWAYS POSSIBLE TO LEARN
MORE, GROW MORE, AND DREAM BIGGER.

I
F THIS BOOK LEAVES YOU WITH
a more positive frame of mind about what lies ahead, then my purpose
for writing it has been fulfilled, and I am gratified. I sincerely appreciate
the time you have spent reading it, and I hope you have found the
exercises beneficial.

As I described to you in Consideration 1, what I consider to have
been a quantum leap in my own personal development occurred when I
stepped behind a velvet rope, met an exceptional man named Philip, and
learned the basis of his mind-set. My conversations and time with Philip
fueled my hunger for further answers and proved to me that there is *no
such thing as dreaming too big.* That was when my hunt began, and from
then on I began finding workable ideas and principles that I believe can
speed anyone along the path to personal fulfillment.

Although I have come by the truths in this book via various routes—
the stories of successful individuals I've met, advice I've been given
and tried, books I've read, and my own personal experiences, both

successes and failures, among them—I have come to realize that Philip's superlative mind-set is essentially a synthesis of these very same beliefs and truths. In fact, it has become clear to me that the vast majority of people who are achieving true success, value, and meaning in their lives either intuitively understand and apply most of the principles shared here or immediately recognize these truths when they encounter them and consciously incorporate them into their daily lives.

The single most inspiring lesson I learned from Philip is the subject of Consideration 1: *keep hunting*. He urged me to discover what holds the greatest meaning in my own life, become intimately familiar with my inherent passions, and then master whatever is important to me. He admonished me to do whatever I do well, then to use the inevitable fruits of my labor for the benefit of others.

For full disclosure, I'll let you know I have encountered techniques during my hunt that I found completely unworkable as well as ones that, even through my best efforts, did not seem to increase my likelihood for success. These I have unceremoniously discarded. What you have read are practical techniques and principles that will align you with the proper mind-set that will help you build significance and ensure your success.

There is always room for more growth, more learning, and bigger dreams. Always be alert to the wisdom that surrounds you. Soak it up as it comes your way. If wisdom does not naturally find you, begin hunting for answers—rediscover more timeless truths for yourself. And, no matter what you are looking for, know that there is no such thing as dreaming too big.

May the cup of your life overflow, my friend, and most sincerely, *"May You Drink from the Saucer."*

FURTHER READING

PERHAPS THE BEST PRESCRIPTION for nurturing a mind-set that will bring value, meaning, and significance into your life—and to the lives of others—is a steady diet of ideas from successful, positive-minded, world class thinkers. Consider the following list of important works by extraordinary men and women. Their words have had a resoundingly positive influence on my life and on the lives of millions of others throughout the world.

Through these writings, you will find inspiration to keep hunting, learning, growing, and dreaming. Many are classics in the personal development field and can be found online, at your local library, and in your local bookstore. Each is full of useful information you can use to shorten your learning curve and accelerate your growth curve. I urge you to explore any that appeal to you. You will be rewarded handsomely for your efforts.

The Art of War by Sun Tzu

As a Man Thinketh by James Allen

Better Than Good: Creating a Life You Can't Wait to Live
by Zig Ziglar

Developing the Leader within You by John C. Maxwell

Endurance: The Greatest Adventure Story Ever Told by Alfred Lansing

Enjoy Every Sandwich: Living Each Day as If It Were Your Last
by Lee Lipsenthal

The Go-Giver: A Little Story about a Powerful Business Idea
by Bob Burg and John David Mann

*Good to Great: Why Some Companies Make the Leap...and
Others Don't* by Jim Collins

The Greatest Salesman in the World by Og Mandino

Happiness on 7 Dollars a Week: A Formula for Living
by Harley B. Bernstein

*Hardwiring Excellence: Purpose, Worthwhile Work, Making a
Difference* by Quint Studer

How to Win Friends and Influence People by Dale Carnegie

The Last Lecture by Randy Pausch with Jeffrey Zaslow

Lincoln the Unknown by Dale Carnegie

*The Millionaire Next Door: The Surprising Secrets of America's
Wealthy* by Thomas J. Stanley and William D. Danko

*Never Eat Alone: And Other Secrets to Success, One Relationship
at a Time* by Keith Ferrazzi

Never Give In! The Best of Winston Churchill's Speeches
by Winston Churchill

*The One Minute Entrepreneur: The Secret to Creating and
Sustaining a Successful Business* by Ken Blanchard,
Don Hutson, and Ethan Willis

The One Minute Negotiator: Simple Steps to Reach Better Agreements by Don Hutson and George Lucas

The Power of Positive Thinking by Norman Vincent Peale

Primal Leadership: Learning to Lead with Emotional Intelligence by Daniel Goleman, Richard E. Boyatzis, and Annie McKee

Rich Dad, Poor Dad: What the Rich Teach Their Kids about Money That the Poor and Middle Class Do Not! by Robert T. Kiyosaki with Sharon L. Lechter

The Richest Man in Babylon by George S. Clason

The 7 Habits of Highly Effective People by Stephen R. Covey

Steve Jobs by Walter Isaacson

Team of Rivals: The Political Genius of Abraham Lincoln by Doris Kearns Goodwin

Think and Grow Rich by Napolean Hill

Trump: The Way to the Top: The Best Business Advice I Ever Received by Donald Trump

Tuesdays with Morrie: An Old Man, a Young Man, and Life's Greatest Lesson by Mitch Albom

Walden; or, Life in the Woods by Henry David Thoreau

Who Moved My Cheese? An Amazing Way to Deal with Change in Your Work and in Your Life by Spencer Johnson and Ken Blanchard

Why Not? Your Best Years Are Yet to Come! by Attila Varga with Bob Proctor

The Wizard of Menlo Park: How Thomas Alva Edison Invented the Modern World by Randall E. Stross

Wooden: A Lifetime of Observations and Reflections On and Off the Court by John Wooden with Steve Jamison

You Were Born Rich by Bob Proctor

APPENDIX

As promised in Consideration 4 (The Scale of Life), my friend and mentor Brian Heath shares his essay here. In it, he relates (in his own words) a transformative experience that has brought considerable significance and meaning to his life.

My Picasso
BY BRIAN HEATH

One

When your focus is on what you don't have, rather than on what you do, life gets out of whack in a hurry. Growing up with a sense of lack moved me in that direction. My desire to alter that feeling only made "getting" seem more important as I got older. I could picture who I thought I wanted to be and what it would look like when I arrived, but how to get there was a mystery. There were many examples, near and far, of those who seemed to know the secret, but they did me no good. In time, I had acquired all the basics of a successful life, but I was sure there was something more, so I kept looking.

As long as I can remember, I've had a fascination with stories of "near-death experiences." Those who have died and come back often relate a story of profound and deeply positive life changes. They instantly became appreciative for their life and circumstances, although nothing else had changed. An easy calm seems to surround them. That was how I wanted to feel. In my late twenties, I used to joke that I would pay ten thousand dollars to have a near-death experience of my own. In fact, I meant it. No surprise, I suppose, considering the way I viewed my life. To me it was the kind of change worth dying for.

I think I always had a sense that I would need some grand event to shake me up and transform me into the person I wanted to be. Little did I know, not only would I get my grand event but, at least initially, the experience would be shattering. Worse still, it would include a terrible cost shared by those I loved. And so I lived my life, oblivious to the truth all around me.

Fast-forward twenty years, and at the age of forty-eight things looked pretty good. I had managed somehow to survive and even thrive. I had a beautiful wife, two beautiful daughters, and an awesome home to call my own. People liked me for the most part. I was a relatively successful salesperson, and my life was "good." Outwardly I tried to give the appearance of being happy. Inwardly I struggled to really appreciate my life. It didn't make sense. What was missing? Why wasn't all of this more than enough?

I've heard that even if one buys a Picasso and hangs it on the wall with great fanfare, in time one will walk by and barely notice it's there. That was me. My life and everything I had was a Picasso in all the important ways. I, however, was too busy looking for that missing piece to realize it.

When my grand event finally did arrive, it shook me to my core. It also started me on my way to a place that had always been in my grasp, had I been aware enough to notice. It still chokes me up that my children had to lose so much for me to see the light, but we reap what we sow. That's a truth that you can't run from. Sadly, it was necessary for me to realize what was truly important in life, and to discover all the unopened gifts that I'd been given.

Two

It was a late spring day almost three years ago when my wife stood across the kitchen from me and said, "I've decided I want a divorce." After those words pounded my ears everything became a blur. It was immediately clear, however, both in her eyes and in her voice, that this time she meant it. That was the first blow. I knew without question that a heavy door had just slammed shut behind me, and although not physically injured, I was facing my very own near-death experience. Unlike the other riveting stories I had been so fond of hearing before, this one was wrenching. I don't know which was worse at that moment, the panic I felt or the overwhelming sense of doom. Either which way, I felt like I was falling, and it wasn't into a warm and guiding light. From that very moment, everything about my life changed forever. All the BS fell away as I looked head-on at what felt like my own demise. As I took in those words, my well-practiced self-importance suddenly looked pitifully pretentious. Every detailed lecture I'd made about some shortcoming seemed painfully immature now. The many lost opportunities to be loving, and what all that would have meant, cascaded through my mind. I was literally coming apart.

There's a surreal quality to an experience like that. It's so shocking that you think it can't really be happening and just real enough so you know there's no going back. As the starkness of my new reality settled in over the months that followed, regret became my partner. I won't bore you with the gamut of emotions I proceeded to experience. It would be enough to say that the sounds that would come from me when the ache became unbearable were otherworldly.

It's been two and a half years since that fateful day. I have traveled an often lonely but enlightening road on my way to figuring a few things out, including one that surprised me the most. As it turned out, the secret I had been looking for all along was not what I'd expected. I, like many out there, had been looking for the epiphany. The one person who could clue me in. The book that would reveal it all. Whatever it was that would magically change me into the person I'd always wanted to be. In the end, what I found was a different kind of secret. After forty-eight years and an ocean of tears, the "secret," as it turned out, was that *there wasn't a secret at all!*

There was no epiphany. No big moment. After all my searching and all the introspection, the so-called secret was just to make a shift in what I chose to see. A choice to look at what was right with things, rather than what was wrong with them. A choice to appreciate what *is,* and let it be enough for the moment. A choice to love in each moment, rather than judge.

Had I ever heard that before? Of course I had. I'd read all the books. Went to hear countless speakers who spoke of what I wanted. I had listened to everyone, including those who died and came back, but I had missed it every time. I had been sure it was going to be a bigger moment of insight, not some minor understanding of a longtime truth. From my own perspective, there was never a person more oblivious than I was. Not one.

Simply put, my lack of appreciation for what I did have had had an extremely corrosive effect on my life. In the end, that cost me something I held very dear. When I finally discovered that my only real "lack" was a lack of gratitude, I started to see that what I thought was missing was only just waiting to be recognized. When I started to get my brain around that, my life started to mean something. It wasn't so much about changing what I believed as it was about changing what I noticed. Two summers ago I also changed the license plate on my car to GRTFL. I have been trying to live it ever since.

Of course the understanding of any insight is just a ticket to look through the window. To step inside and experience what's available with a focus on Gratitude is still a choice. It's a moment-by-moment choice that can be passed up just as easily as any other opportunity that comes your way. But you can choose it over and over until it becomes a habit. At first it can feel completely unnatural, especially after a life of being self-absorbed. Probably a little like driving in England. You may know that you're supposed to drive on the left side of the road, but that doesn't mean you don't find yourself wanting to get back over on the other side. But over time it can get to the point where it starts to feel natural. I still catch myself slipping at times, but little things make me feel like I'm headed in the right direction.

Three

Today one of those many "little things" happened. It's what prompted me, two and a half years since my "near-death experience," to be writing about my life in this New York City airport.

It all started with missing my connection today. When I'd arrived at the gate, the ticket agent told me the next flight I'd hoped to be on was sold out. She looked and looked for my next-best option, but could only find a flight much later that night. I could tell that she had really tried. When I thanked her for that, she knew I meant it and gave me a smile. I booked the later flight and had already walked to another part of the airport when I thought I heard my name over the intercom. I listened as it was repeated. "Brian Heath, please return to Gate Number One." Yes, that was me. Surprised, I hurried back.

When I got there the ticket lady said, "I kept looking for your name after you left, and noticed that somehow you are already booked on an earlier flight." I don't know why she had kept on looking, but I really thanked her this time as she handed me my new ticket. I would now be home a full three hours earlier.

And then it happened. I hadn't walked away more than twenty steps this time when I started to well up. It just came. Right there at Gate Number One in the middle of JFK and hundreds of other travelers. As I wiped away the unexpected tears, I knew where they were coming from. My focus on "getting" had begun to fade and was being replaced with an appreciation of what really matters. I had changed.

I know the old me probably would have been muttering, "It's about time I caught a break," but the new me was just plain grateful. So here I sit marooned in an airport, with an overwhelming feeling that life doesn't get any better than this. It's just more proof to me that it's noticing the little things in life that make a life worthwhile. Somehow I know this won't be the last time I notice. There's too much goodness going on in any life and far too little time to waste on pretense.

Epilogue

I still remember well the years I spent stumbling along with my back to the window. It's hard to imagine sometimes, how often I failed to see the goodness all around me. I've come to like the fact, however, that what's good and what's true in life won't ever shout at you. It's just there for you to notice whenever you're ready. There's something spiritual about that that I can't really describe. More and more, it seems to me that what is truly great in life only ever *whispers*.

There's a real choice to be made that comes right before every action we take, every word that we say, and every thought we think. We can go negative or we can go positive, each and every time. It really doesn't matter what we're faced with; we can choose to see what's good about it if we want to. And before you come up with something so terrible that there just couldn't be something good in it, you should know there are those who have already experienced each of the examples you'd cite, and found a way to pry the goodness from its terrible grip on them. Life is full of these stories if you take the time to notice. I've lived one myself. They are literally everywhere.

I know now that what I had before my life came apart was everything that I'd ever wanted. To lose it was a gut-wrenching experience, one I could not even face for over a year. It's a loss that can never be made whole, but the incredible goodness of life has been made clear in its wake. I've come to this. If I were left destitute, hated, and on my deathbed wracked in pain, the incredible blessings I have, in the form of my two beautiful daughters alone, would be more than enough for me to smile toward heaven every day with gratitude. There is an answer to "What's good about this?" in every situation life brings. But you have to look for it. You pass on each of these opportunities at your own peril.

I think everyone who searches eventually comes to the same conclusion. What we're looking for in life, what we often think is missing, has been with us all along. We come into this world with every bit of it in place, ready to be enjoyed. The sooner we acknowledge it, the sooner we can stop chasing "secrets." And when that happens, there isn't enough time in the day to ponder what's missing. The truth of what we really have and the well of goodness we all possess can then take center stage.

I never got my family back, and the regret I came to know is still there in the quiet moments, but the experiences I've had since discovering the so called "secret" have been life changing. The new me, together with my family and all that we had, would have noticed the important things and been Grateful for all of them. *The new me would have noticed my priceless Picasso every day.*

What you should do is up to you. Hopefully you're wiser than me, and you not only appreciate what you have but are sure to let those around you know it often. That will change more than just "your" life. And so I'll leave you with one more thing I now know for sure: the truth of these things is inescapable.

"If you're not grateful for what you have, you will never be happy with what you want."

As promised in Consideration 7 (Ask How and Ask It Now—*Charge!*), I am sharing Joshua Chamberlain's "The Furling of the Flags" here. With his eloquent writing style, Chamberlain brings us back in time and into the heat of the moment.

The Furling of the Flags
BY JOSHUA LAWRENCE CHAMBERLAIN

It was now the morning of the 12th of April. I had been ordered to have my lines formed for the ceremony at sunrise. It was a chill gray morning, depressing to the senses. But our hearts made warmth. Great memories uprose; great thoughts went forward. We formed along the principal street, from the bluff bank of the stream to near the Court House on the left,—to face the last line of battle, and receive the last remnant of the arms and colors of that great army which ours had been created to confront for all that death can do for life. We were remnants also: Massachusetts, Maine, Michigan, Maryland, Pennsylvania, New York; veterans, and replaced veterans; cut to pieces, cut down, consolidated, divisions into brigades, regiments into one, gathered by State origin; this little line, quintessence or metempsychosis of Porter's old corps of Gaines' Mill and Malvern Hill; men of near blood born, made nearer by blood shed. Those facing us—now, thank God! the same.

As for me, I was once more with my old command. But this was not all I needed. I had taken leave of my little First Brigade so endeared to me, and the end of the fighting had released the Second from all orders from me. But these deserved to share with me now as they had so faithfully done in the sterner passages of the campaign. I got permission from General Griffin to have them also in the parade. I placed the First Brigade in line a little to our rear, and the Second on the opposite side of the street facing us and leaving ample space for the movements of the coming ceremony. Thus the whole division was out, and under my direction for the occasion, although I was not the division commander. I thought this troubled General Bartlett a little, but he was a manly and soldierly man and made no comment. He contented himself by mounting his whole staff and with the division flag riding around our lines and conversing as he found opportunity with the Confederate officers. This in no manner disturbed me; my place and part were definite and clear.

Our earnest eyes scan the busy groups on the opposite slopes, breaking camp for the last time, taking down their little shelter-tents and folding them carefully as precious things, then slowly forming ranks as for unwelcome duty. And now they move. The dusky swarms forge forward into gray columns of march. On they come, with the old swinging route step and swaying battle-flags. In the van, the proud Confederate ensign—the great field of white with canton of star-strewn cross of blue on a field of red, the regimental battle-flags with the same escutcheon following on, crowded so thick, by thinning out of men, that the whole column seemed crowned with red. At the right of our line our little group mounted beneath our flags, the red Maltese cross on a field of white, erewhile so bravely borne through many a field more crimson than itself, its mystic meaning now ruling all.

The momentous meaning of this occasion impressed me deeply. I resolved to mark it by some token of recognition, which could be no other than a salute of arms. Well aware of the responsibility assumed, and of the criticisms that would follow, as the sequel proved, nothing of that kind could move me in the least. The act could be defended, if needful, by the suggestion that such a salute was not to the cause for which the flag of the Confederacy stood, but to its going down before the flag of the Union. My main reason, however, was one for which I sought no authority nor asked forgiveness. Before us in proud humiliation stood the embodiment of manhood: men whom neither toils and sufferings, nor the fact of death, nor disaster, nor hopelessness could bend from their resolve; standing before us now, thin, worn, and famished, but erect, and with eyes looking level into ours, waking memories that bound us together as no other bond;—was not such manhood to be welcomed back into a Union so tested and assured?

Instructions had been given; and when the head of each division column comes opposite our group, our bugle sounds the signal and instantly our whole line from right to left, regiment by regiment in succession, gives the soldiers salutation, from the "order arms" to the old "carry"—the marching salute. Gordon at the head of the column, riding with heavy spirit and downcast face, catches the sound of shifting arms, looks up, and, taking the meaning, wheels superbly, making with himself and his horse one uplifted figure, with profound salutation as he drops the point of his sword to the boot toe; then facing to his own command, gives word for his successive brigades to pass us with the same position of the manual,—honor answering honor. On our part not a sound of trumpet more, nor roll of drum; not a cheer, nor word nor whisper of vain-glorying, nor motion of man standing again at the order, but an awed stillness rather, and breath-holding, as if it were the passing of the dead!

As each successive division masks our own, it halts, the men face inward towards us across the road, twelve feet away; then carefully "dress" their line, each captain taking pains for the good appearance of his company, worn and half starved as they were. The field and staff take their positions in the intervals of regiments; generals in rear of their commands. They fix bayonets, stack arms; then, hesitatingly, remove cartridge-boxes and lay them down. Lastly,—reluctantly, with agony of expression,—they tenderly fold their flags, battle-worn and torn, blood-stained, heart-holding colors, and lay them down; some frenziedly rushing from the ranks, kneeling over them, clinging to them, pressing them to their lips with burning tears. And only the Flag of the Union greets the sky!

What visions thronged as we looked into each other's eyes! Here pass the men of Antietam, the Bloody Lane, the Sunken Road, the Cornfield, the Burnside-Bridge; the men whom Stonewall Jackson on the second night at Fredericksburg begged Lee to let him take and crush the two corps of the Army of the Potomac huddled in the streets in darkness and confusion; the men who swept away the Eleventh Corps at Chancellorsville; who left six thousand of their companions around the bases of Culp's and Cemetery Hills at Gettysburg; these survivors of the terrible Wilderness, the Bloody-Angle at Spottsylvania, the slaughter pen of Cold Harbor, the whirlpool of Bethesda Church!

Here comes Cobb's Georgia Legion, which held the stone wall on Marye's Heights at Fredericksburg, close before which we piled our dead for breastworks so that the living might stay and live.

Here too come Gordon's Georgians and Hoke's North Carolinians, who stood before the terrific mine explosion at Petersburg, and advancing retook the smoking crater and the dismal heaps of dead—ours more than theirs—huddled in the ghastly chasm.

Here are the men of McGowan, Hunton, and Scales, who broke the Fifth Corps lines on the White Oak Road, and were so desperately driven back on that forlorn night of March 31st by my thrice-decimated brigade.

Now comes Anderson's Fourth Corps, only Bushrod Johnson's Division left, and this the remnant of those we fought so fiercely on the Quaker Road two weeks ago, with Wises Legion, too fierce for its own good.

Here passes the proud remnant of Ransom's North Carolinians which we swept through Five Forks ten days ago,—and all the little that was left of this division in the sharp passages at Sailor's Creek five days thereafter.

Now makes its last front A. P. Hill's old Corps, Heth now at the head, since Hill had gone too far forward ever to return: the men who poured destruction into our division at Shepardstown Ford, Antietam, in 1862, when Hill reported the Potomac running blue with our bodies; the men who opened the desperate first day's fight at Gettysburg, where withstanding them so stubbornly our Robinson's Brigades lost 1185 men, and the Iron Brigade alone 1153,—these men of Heth's Division here too losing 2850 men, companions of these now looking into our faces so differently.

What is this but the remnant of Mahone's Division, last seen by us at the North Anna? Its thinned ranks of worn, bright-eyed men recalling scenes of costly valor and ever-remembered history.

Now the sad great pageant—Longstreet and his men! What shall we give them for greeting that has not already been spoken in volleys of thunder and written in lines of fire on all the riverbanks of Virginia? Shall we go back to Gaines' Mill and Malvern Hill? Or to the Antietam of Maryland, or Gettysburg of Pennsylvania?—deepest graven of all. For here is what remains of Kershaw's Division, which left 40 per cent. of its men at Antietam, and at Gettysburg with Barksdale's and Semmes' Brigades tore through the Peach Orchard, rolling up the right of our gallant Third Corps, sweeping over the proud batteries of Massachusetts—Bigelow and Philips,—where under the smoke we saw the earth brown and blue with prostrate bodies of horses and men, and the tongues of overturned cannon and caissons pointing grim and stark in the air.

Then in the Wilderness, at Spottsylvania and thereafter, Kershaw's Division again, in deeds of awful glory, held their name and fame, until fate met them at Sailor's Creek, where Kershaw himself, and Ewell, and so many more, gave up their arms and hopes,—all, indeed, but manhood's honor.

With what strange emotion I look into these faces before which in the mad assault on Rives' Salient, June 18, 1864, I was left for dead under their eyes! It is by miracles we have lived to see this day,—any of us standing here.

Now comes the sinewy remnant of fierce Hood's Division, which at Gettysburg we saw pouring through the Devil's Den, and the Plum Run gorge; turning again by the left our stubborn Third Corps, then swarming up the rocky bastions of Round Top, to be met there by equal valor, which changed Lee's whole plan of battle and perhaps the story of Gettysburg.

Ah, is this Pickett's Division?—this little group left of those who on the lurid last day of Gettysburg breasted level cross-fire and thunderbolts of storm, to be strewn back drifting wrecks, where after that awful, futile, pitiful charge we buried them in graves a furlong wide, with names unknown!

Met again in the terrible cyclone-sweep over the breast-works at Five Forks; met now, so thin, so pale, purged of the mortal,—as if knowing pain or joy no more. How could we help falling on our knees, all of us together, and praying God to pity and forgive us all!

Thus, all day long, division after division comes and goes, surrendered arms being removed by our wagons in the intervals, the cartridge-boxes emptied in the street when the ammunition was found unserviceable, our men meanwhile resting in place.

ACKNOWLEDGMENTS

Mom—For your unconditional love and unrivaled support

Dad—For being more than just a father and for being part of every life event

Amy—For being the sister any boy or man would be proud to call his own

Nana and Grampy—For always being there and for being my best friends

Nana Arbour—For your kind soul and dedication to family

Tabatha—For your love, loyalty, and enduring support

Haleigh—For being my "Little One"

My friends—You know who you are, and I love you all

Brian Heath—For your honest and humble perspective

Harry Lanphear III—For your strategery and camaraderie

Connie Fotakis—For memorable talks on the lake and for helping me build a team

Dan Koon—For your strong enthusiasm toward this project

Carrie Cook—For your constant availability and for always being an outstanding listener

Bill Gove Jr.—For your friendship and consistent encouragement

Matthew Stein—For your organizational support in all areas of this project

Amy Chamberlain—For giving this book its "polish"

My teachers and professors—For sharing your wisdom

All my sports coaches—For always pushing me to raise the bar, to work hard, and to play hard

The people of Kennebec Valley—For providing an environment in which one can flourish

Don Hutson—For your generosity, integrity, and trust in me

Terri Murphy—For your friendship and unique connection

Danny Cox—For your time, insight, and hospitality

To those who read my books—For your time; it is a coin